The Logic of Religion

The Logic
of Religion

by
Joseph M. Bochenski, O.P.

New York University Press/1965

The Reverend Charles Force Deems, born in 1820, was deeply concerned with the relationship of science and philosophy to religion. In 1881 he founded the American Institute of Christian Philosophy for the investigation of the most significant questions pertaining to the relationship. In 1895, two years after the death of Dr. Deems, the American Institute of Christian Philosophy endowed a "Lectureship of Philosophy" at New York University in his honor and for a continuation of the purpose for which the American Institute of Christian Philosophy had been founded.

Father Bochenski's lectures were sponsored by the Deems Fund.

Preface

A book on logic of religion must, by its very title, cause some surprise; it may even be somewhat shocking. Although the legitimacy of a logic of religion is one of the major questions discussed in the body of the present work, it will perhaps be useful to try to dispel at once some of the misunderstandings which might be caused by the title. First, no proof of or apology for religion is offered; in other words, no attempt will be made to justify the correctness of any beliefs. Second, a full philosophy of religion will not be supplied; only such aspects of it will be studied as are accessible to logic — and, it must be added, to logic at its present stage of development; for we do not as yet possess sufficient logical tools to analyze fully even those aspects of religion. Third, the contention that the logical aspects of religion are the most important aspects is not made here; it is simply claimed, and an attempt is made to justify this claim, that there are such aspects, whatever their relevance might be. And, finally, no formalization of religious discourse is supplied; only people who do not know what a formalized system really is may doubt this.

The author is very much aware that he is working in a relatively unexplored field. Not that there does not exist in different theologies and Buddhologies an ample literature on most of the problems

v

touched upon here, but the tradition of such research has been broken and, with the exception of
the problems of meaning, the author found himself in a situation not dissimilar to that described
by Aristotle at the end of the *Topics*. Also, so far as
he knows, no attempt has ever been made to formulate a general logic of religion applicable to all
great religions rather than to a particular religion.
This is said not to praise the author's work but instead to offer some mitigating circumstances to
explain its inadequacy and to appeal for that in-
dulgence which the Founder of Logic himself felt
compelled to ask for.

For the inadequacies are many. The book describes the idea of a logic of religion rather than
offering a complete system; if a limited number of
problems—and certainly not all problems—are
mentioned, few are resolved. Moreover, whatever
is supplied here belongs to that stage of difficult
and not very satisfactory thinking which precedes
formalization.

An effort has been made to keep the text in the
body of the book as untechnical as possible. However, the reader who is not familiar with the current terminology of logic and semantics must be
warned that many terms are used here as they are
in the context of those sciences and not in the sense
they may have elsewhere. To illustrate this by one
example: the author was amazed when a learned
theologian declared to him that a meaningful sentence is necessarily true. Obviously, by "meaningful" he meant something quite different from what
logicians usually do. It is doubtful if the reading
of the present book would be of any utility to that
particular scholar.

No quotations and references are to be found in the book. It seemed to the author that they would be out of place in a purely speculative (that is, non-historical) work. Some philosophers are mentioned, but it was not thought useful to indicate where, for example, Kant spoke about his postulates or Tarski discussed the concept of truth.

The content of the present book is a re-elaboration of a series of lectures which the author had the privilege of delivering in March, 1963, at New York University. The same topics later formed the subject of lectures at Fribourg, Basel, Amsterdam, and Utrecht. Each of these lectures was followed by discussion. The author wishes to express his thanks to the Committee of the Charles F. Deems Lectures and to all those scholars who made suggestions during the discussions.

J. M. BOCHENSKI, O.P.

Main Abbreviations

"BD" for "basic dogma" (Section 19)
"OR" for "object of religion"
"PD" for "profane discourse"
"RD" for "religious discourse"
"TD" for "total discourse"
"π" for "the class of profane sentences"
"ρ" for "the class of sentences belonging to the objective faith" (Section 19)
"$\tau'\rho$" for "the class of sentences derived from the elements of ρ" (Section 24)
Instead of "elements of π" the expression "π-sentences" is used, and similarly for "ρ" and "$\tau'\rho$."

Remark on Semantic Terminology

No semantic term is intentionally used in this book as presupposing any philosophy. Thus, when speaking about "meaning," it is not supposed that meanings are separated entities, etc. The same is true of the expression "proposition." The term "expresses" is often used whenever it is not desirable to make a distinction between meaning, reference, and so on.

Contents

Preface   *v*

Abbreviations and Semantic Terminology   *viii*

I   *Introduction*   *1*
    1. On general logic
    2. On applied logic
    3. On religion
    4. On logic of religion
    5. Logic of religion and theology
    6. The program of logic of religion

II *Religion and Logic*   *19*
    7. On the history of the relations between logic and religion
    8. The problem of a logic of religion
    9. On meaning
    10. Theories of religion
    11. On the Unspeakable
    12. On communicativeness in RD
    13. On religious propositions
    14. On the universality of logic
    15. On the universality of semantics
    16. On dialectics and its use in logic of religion

III *The Structure of Religious Discourse*   *52*
    17. On the formal structure of a discourse and its problems
    18. On the structural problems of RD
    19. On the general structure of RD
    20. On the axiomatization of ρ
    21. On the logical syntax of "God"
    22. On the logical relations between π and ρ

23. On $\pi \cap \rho$

24. On $-\pi \cap -\rho$

25. On formal logic of $\tau'\rho$

26. The structure of TD

27. On inconsistencies in RD

28. Para-religious discourse

IV *Meaning in Religious Discourse*   89

29. Semantics of RD and hermeneutics of the Scriptures

30. The problems of meaning in RD

31. On meaning and verification

32. On indirect verifiability of ρ-sentences by authority

33. On indirect verification of ρ-sentences by reduction

34. On direct verification of ρ-sentences

35. On Mystery

36. Negative Theology

37. On Analogy

V *Justification of Religious Discourse*   118

38. On justification

39. On authority

40. The problem of justification of RD

41. Theories of justification

42. On the blind leap

43. On Rationalism

44. The trust theory

45. The deductivist theory

46. The authority theory

47. On crisis of authority

48. On the religious hypothesis

49. Problems of the religious hypothesis

VI *Appendix*   156

50. Analysis of Analogy

51. Analysis of Authority
    Registers.

Indexes   175

The Logic of Religion

I

Introduction

In this general introduction the idea of the logic of religion (abbreviated as "LR") will be described and its main classes of problems stated. In order to do this, we shall have to enquire into the meaning of "logic" (Section 1); then we shall examine the concept of applied logic and the conditions of existence of such a logic (Section 2). This having been done, a similar analysis will be performed on "religion" (Section 3) followed by an examination of the concept of LR (Section 4) and its relation to theology particularly with respect to Buddhology (Section 5). Finally, a program for LR will be established (Section 6).

1. On general logic

The term "logic" has many different uses, and it is notoriously difficult to supply a convenient analytic definition of it. But if we limit ourselves to what is being really carried out now under that name in Western Europe and in the United States, we shall find that, if not a definition, at least a description of what is meant by "logic" is not impossible. As a matter of fact, there are at least four sorts of studies which used to be called "logic" in the broad meaning of the term. They are: Formal Logic, Semiotics, Methodology, and Philosophy of Logic.

1.1

1. Formal logic. By formal logic is meant the study of some very general laws, namely, those in which, in addition to variables, only so-called logical functors occur. What a logical functor is may be best determined by listing the basic (undefined) functors of the present-day systems. Among them are Sheffer's functor, the existential quantifier, and similars. Another way of describing formal logic is to refer to some classical work on it, such as the *Prior Analytics* of Aristotle or Frege's *Begriffschrift*.

2. Semiotics. By semiotics is meant the most general analysis of symbols. If this analysis is carried on by logical (that is, formal-logical) tools, semiotics is a part of logic, in the broader meaning of the word. It is, in a way, applied logic; but at least some parts of logical semiotics are so strictly connected with formal logic itself that they have always been studied by formal logicians for the sake of their formal-logical enquiry. Therefore, semiotics is considered a part of general logic. It is divided, traditionally, into syntax, semantics, and pragmatics, of which semantics is perhaps of greatest relevance to many logical studies.

3. Methodology. This is the study of the applications of formal-logical laws and rules to the practice of science and possibly to other fields of human activities. While special methodologies of concrete fields are usually studied in the respective sciences, general methodology has been, since Aristotle, part of logic in the broad meaning of the term.

4. Philosophy of logic. Aside from the three disciplines mentioned above, there is still the study of logic itself and of some basic questions concerned with its foundations and relations to other sciences. This is usually termed "philosophy of logic" and is also usually carried on by logicians.

The logical order of these disciplines is such that formal logic appears as basic; all other logical disciplines presuppose it. However, in formal logic some principles of semantics and of methodology (methodology of deduction) are used. This is the reason why the first three disciplines together form one science, general logic.

General logic thus described has two outstanding characteristics: it is concerned with discourse and with objective structures.

1.2.1 A. LOGIC IS CONCERNED WITH DISCOURSE. In the whole history of logic, formal or otherwise, there is no known case of any serious study which has not been carried out on the basis of some discourse. It is true that some philosophers (especially since Descartes) have talked about the study of concepts "in themselves"; however, logicians have always dealt with concepts as expressed by words, that is, with discourse. This tradition started with Plato and is still absolutely general. There seem to have been two principal reasons for adopting this method. (1) Concepts do not subsist in themselves (as against Cartesian mythology) but are meanings of terms; therefore, they should be studied through the terms, that is, through discourse. (2) Written (or spoken) terms are material things (or events)—and it is a basic methodological principle that, whenever it is possible, we should start with such things (or events), because they are much easier to study than mental entities.

This does not mean, of course, that the logician is concerned with discourse only. On the contrary, his interest is directed toward meaningful discourse, and not toward the material terms alone. But in practice he always deals with discourse.

1.2.2   B. LOGIC IS ABOUT OBJECTIVE STRUCTURES. There is a practically unanimous consensus among logicians that they are primarily dealing with some of the most general structures of objects, and not with subjective acts of the mind. It is true that the general rules of correct thinking can be immediately derived from some logical laws; but these laws are certainly not about mental activities. For example, when a logician states that, if no *A* is *B*, then no *B* is *A*, he is not talking about the rules of reasoning but, at least primarily, he is establishing a necessary connection between two states of things.

In order to avoid misunderstandings the following remark may be made. This is not a book on philosophy of logic, and an explicit position as to the different philosophical theories of logic does not need to be taken here. Therefore, the terms used—even if they seem to be drawn from a particular philosophy of logic—may be interpreted according to the reader's own views. This may be illustrated by the following example. We constantly talk about meaning. Now the term "meaning" itself is completely neutral with regard to philosophies of logic. Some philosophies of logic assume that there are entities called "meanings"; others assume that there is nothing of the sort. Yet even the latter have to make a distinction between meaningful and meaningless discourse—and such a distinction alone is presupposed here, not any particular interpretation of "meaning."

The same applies to the term "expresses," which will often be used in what follows. It has been chosen because of its apparent neutrality. We shall therefore say that a term *t* expresses something if and only if it conveys something to the user of *t*. Thus, "expresses" may be understood as "denotes," "means," etc. An effort has been made in this work to remain as neutral as possible toward such specifications.

2. On applied logic

Applied logic is to be distinguished from pure or general logic. It consists, as the name indicates, in the application of pure logic to a certain extra-logical field.

However, logic can be applied to a field, say *f*, in two different ways:

1. Every field in which there is any reasoning, ordering of sentences, etc., may be said to be applied logic. What is meant, then, is that some portions of formal logic are used, and that some extra-logical terms, axioms, and, perhaps, rules are added. In this sense, for example, contemporary physics or any sort of theology is applied logic. However, this is not the proper use of the term.

2. Second, we may mean by "applied logic" the study of those logical laws and rules (including the laws and rules of semantics and methodology) which are used in a given field. This differs from one field to another. It has been shown, for example by Professor Woodger, that biology uses some parts of formal logic which are hardly ever considered by the mathematician; and Professor von Wright and others have elaborated systems of modal logic, especially needed — according to them — in the field of morals. Another instance may be historiography, which is notorious for its use of many sorts of weak implication. The study of such peculiar parts of logic — which very often have to be developed *ad hoc* — is applied logic in the proper meaning of the term.

The following question occurs in connection with the concept of applied logic: under what conditions can there be an applied logic of a field? The answer is readily supplied by the two general properties of pure logic. It may be formulated in the following theorem:

2.1   *For all* f: *if* f *is a field of human activity, then there is applied logic of* f *if and only if* f *includes discourse which embodies or expresses some objective structures.*

It must be stressed that this theorem contains as its main functor an equivalence; therefore it has far-reaching consequences which appear to open wider possibilities to applied logic than those considered by logicians up to now.

As a matter of fact, the historical situation in Western logic has been this: it has practically always been developed for the sake of science and especially of mathematics. This was the case with Plato, with Aristotle in his *Posterior Analytics*, and finally with Whitehead and Russell. But science is uniquely interested in propositions. Consequently, the scope of logic, especially formal logic, has been limited to propositions and their parts. Moreover, since in science all propositions which are not logical are factual, logic has been constructed in such a way as to be able to deal with the factual only.

But this is by no means a necessary limitation of logic, at least not where formal logic is concerned. During the twentieth century a broadening of the scope of logic has been carried on in at least two directions. One is the previously mentioned formal logic of morals, that is, of a field in which most formulae are not indicative sentences but imperatives. As to the second, the late lamented Austin convincingly showed that certain formulae – called by him "performatives" – can become the object of a formal-logical study. As is known, these performatives can be neither true nor false, but they have two analogous properties, called by Austin "happiness" and "unhappiness," and nothing forbids the construction of a formal logic for them.

On the other hand, our theorem also shows the limits of applied logic. There can be no applied logic in two cases:

1. Where there is no discourse at all.

2. Where discourse is present, but does not embody or express an objective structure. This may occur in two ways:

a When the discourse is completely meaningless.

b When, although it is meaningful, it expresses only subjective states and not objective structures.

Condition (b) must be mitigated with respect to one part of logic, namely, semantics. There can be semantics of a discourse which conveys only subjective meanings. But neither formal logic nor methodology can be applied to it.

Moreover, for methodology there is one more severe condition: in order to become an object of methodology, the discourse must express not only objective structures but propositions. For methodology is essentially a theory of truth-conditions, and only propositions can be true.

We have now arrived at a more detailed statement of conditions of applied logic:

2.2   *If* f *is a field of human activity, there is applied formal logic of* f *if and only if* f *contains discourse which expresses objective structures:*

2.3   *There is semantics of* f *if and only if there is meaningful discourse in* f.

2.4   *There is methodology of* f *if and only if there is discourse in* f *which expresses, at least in part, propositions.*

3.   On religion

"Religion" is another term which, exactly as is true of "logic," can hardly be defined analytically if all uses of it are concerned. There are simply too many divergent phenomena which are referred to by it. For the scope of the present study it will therefore be necessary to limit the reference of the term to some religions. Here we shall apply the term "religion" only to the so-called great religions of the present, by which we mean Brahmanism, Buddhism, Judaism, Christianity, and Islam. And even the meaning of these religious terms must be restricted to the "great" churches, with exclusion of sects. This is, of course, not an evaluation, but simply a linguistic convention which is thought to be necessary in order to achieve a certain degree of precision with regard to the object of this study.

But even described in this way, religion offers a stupendous multiplicity of aspects. It is, most certainly, a psychological phenomenon and an object of psychology (psychology of religion); it is also a social phenomenon and, as such, it forms the object of sociology (sociology of religion). Further, each of the religions has a discipline of its own, which is called "theology" or (in the case of Hinayana Buddhism) "Buddhology." As to the behavior, linguistic and otherwise, of the believers of religions, it is often very widely different from one religion to another.

However, there are in all religions, as described above, at least a few constant common traits. We may enumerate the following:

3.1   1. Religion is a social phenomenon. By this we mean that it is a complex of events present in human groups. These groups are characterized by a sort of behavior called "religious;" by this we mean that there are common behaviors of the members of such groups.

3.2   2. One outstanding characteristic of this behavior is the use of a particular language, called religious discourse; this expression will be abbreviated here as "RD," or in case of the RD of a religion a as "RD$'a$."

3.3   3. The class of utterances forming RD contains a non-empty subclass which is called the "Creed."

3.4   4. The acceptance of the Creed is of such paramount importance for every religion that a believer of a given religion may be defined by his acceptance of all elements of the corresponding Creed.

Because of the use of "religion" as described above, several kinds of discourse may seem to lie outside the scope of the present research. For example, the discourse of ideologically bound political parties, such as the National Socialist Party or the Communist Party, is outside the scope of this enquiry.

However, even if there are considerable differences between religion, as understood here, and other such phenomena, there is still much that they have in common. As far as, for example, Communism is concerned, its discourse is formally organized in a way very similar to that of religion. Because of this similarity, the present enquiry may be helpful, at least insofar as its formal-logical and methodological parts are concerned, for the understanding of the logic of such other kinds of discourse.

4. On logic of religion

Logic of religion will be, according to what has been said above, logic as applied to religious discourse. In connection with this definition two questions merit brief consideration.

1. What logic should be applied? The answer is that in the establishment of logic of religion there will be two successive stages. The first will consist of the application of such laws and rules of general logic as have already been constituted for general purposes. This will hold true equally of formal logic, semiotics, and methodology. An assumption made here which has still to be examined later on is that

RD is subject to these laws and rules as is any other human discourse. Of course, only the general part of logic is meant, not those parts which were elaborated for some particular purposes. It may happen, indeed, that some peculiar branch of logic, constructed for another field, is also applicable to religion. Yet in each case this must be examined, whereas the general principles of logic are universally valid and applicable.

The second step will presumably consist of the developing of special logical — formal, semiotic, and methodological — tools, which may be needed for the sake of analysis of RD. This is, indeed, what practically always happens when we try to apply logic to an extra-logical field.

It should be stressed that in the present research we will try to do the most we can with conventional logical tools before building up new theories. On the other hand, the field of logical laws and rules being infinite and RD having some very peculiar characteristics, it is *a priori* highly probable that special parts of logic will have to be elaborated for its analysis.

2. *To what material should logic be applied?* The answer is that this material must be the empirically given RD as it is, namely, the discourse factually used by religious communities. This is also the case with other departments of applied logic; for example, logic of biology does not deal with a

discourse conceived *a priori* but with the empirically given discourse of biologists.

This suggests that the situation of applied logic and in particular that of the logic of religion is very different from the status of general logic, which is supposed to be purely *a priori*. This author's opinion is, however, different. He thinks that even general logic is ultimately analysis of some structures embodied in concrete discourse; only general logic deals with structures common to all such discourse, hence the impression that it is *à priori*.

One classical instance taken from the field of semantics will help in understanding the afore-mentioned empirical element in applied logic. This instance is Professor Tarski's well-known definition of truth. This is constructed in the frame of reference of an artificial language established *ad hoc* and is reached with the help of high abstract logical procedures. However, the avowed aim of the author is to supply a definition which fits the meaning of the everyday "true" and, as a matter of fact, a convenient definition of that term is supplied by him. Tarski's procedure will be an ideal for every sort of applied logic and, in particular, for logic of religion.

We meet here, however, with one major difficulty. In order to base our analysis on a solid foundation we would need extensive empirical research in RD and its use within different religious communities. Unfortunately, very few studies of this sort have been conducted and those which are known are not based on the desire to disclose the facts most interesting for the logicians.

But this is not a fatal handicap. In order to perform an analysis of such an abstract character as that used in logic of religion, perhaps it will be sufficient to take into consideration some obvious and universally known features of RD and of the current behavior of the believers. Anyway, given the lack of empirical research in this field, we shall be bound to proceed in this manner.

5. Logic of religion and theology

Historically, logic of religion has been mostly, if not exclusively, cultivated by theologians (and by Buddhologists). However, this does not seem to be more than a historical accident and is by no means connected with the nature of logic of religion.

Theology may be defined as a study in which, along with other axioms, at least one sentence is assumed which belongs to a given Creed and which is not sustained by persons other than the believers of a given religion. It may of course happen that such sentences are recognized as true by the believers of several different religions — nevertheless only believers of some religion do accept them, not other persons.

But no such assumption is needed in order to

study logic of religion. This needs, as a matter of fact, only two classes of assumptions: one is the class of general logical laws and rules; the second is a class of meta-linguistic statements about the concretely existing RD's. For example, the student of logic of religion has to assume that the believers of one or another religion say that God is our father, but he does not need to assume that God is our father; the latter sentence, and this only, is a characteristic assumption of theology.

5.1   It follows that logic of religion is not a part of theology or of Buddhology.

The same thing can also be expressed in the following way: a theologian as such can study only the RD of his religion; but the student of logic of religion is interested in problems which are common to all religions (as described above). Therefore, the student of logic is not, as such, a theologian.

5.2   However, logic of religion is an auxiliary science of theology and it may be even suggested that it is one of its most important auxiliaries. This is not directly evident as long as the theologian attends to his proper business, that is, as long as he works out his religious assumptions, and this in spite of the fact that he then uses logical laws and rules. But it becomes obvious and relevant indeed when a theologian starts reflecting on his own work.

The situation is here somewhat, if not quite, similar to that which we find in science. In science also there is no great need of logic of the field concerned, as long as the scientist is involved in his proper business; but once he starts reflecting about his work, logic of his science becomes of paramount importance. The difference is, however, this: although a scientist is not bound by the nature of his study to reflect, the theologian may be said to be obliged to do so.

It seems, therefore, that logic of religion is relatively more relevant to theology than the logic of sciences is to the sciences.

There is also one peculiar respect in which logic of religion appears to be most useful for theology. It is, namely, that the function of logic of religion consists of analysis of theology itself, that is, of establishing a meta-theological system. It is the logician of religion who shows the theologian what he is doing, what sort of logic he is using, what rules he is applying, and so on. Of course, the logician of religion can do this only in general.

This means that we have to distinguish between general logic of religion and the logic of a particular religion. Yet even the logic of a particular religion does not need to be theology. The first argument stated above to show that general logic of religion is not theology, applies here also: the student of the logic of a particular religion does not need to make any assumption belonging to the Creed of that religion.

In this book only general problems of logic of

religion are considered. It is indeed doubtful if anybody, except a theologian, will be sufficiently interested in the problematic of a particular religion to make enquiries into special logic of religion.

6. The program of logic of religion

1. The first problem logic of religion must face is that of the existence or legitimacy of a logic of religion itself. As there certainly is a RD, at least some sort of semantic analysis of it is always possible. But the question of validity of general rules of semantics must be still examined. Moreover, the question as to the possibility of a formal logic and a methodology of religion is highly controversial and must be examined. This is, therefore, the first task of logic of religion. It corresponds to one of the tasks of philosophy of logic in general logic.

In the course of this discussion it must be asked if there are objective structures communicated by RD and if at least some among them are propositions. Only if both those questions can be answered affirmatively do the subsequent parts of logic of religion become possible. If so, there will be chapters concerned with the following problems.

2. The problem of the logical structure of RD and of its relations to other types of discourse. It is the internal logical problem of religion and belongs partly to formal logic, partly (and above all) to methodology of religion.

3. The problem of meaning in RD. This is a particularly complex and interesting field. Its study constitutes the semantics of religion.

4. Finally, the question of the justification of religious sentences must be considered. This belongs entirely to methodology of religion.

We shall have, consequently, four major parts of logic of religion:

1. On logic of religion itself.
2. On the logical structure of RD.
3. On meaning in RD.
4. On the justification of religious discourse.

II

Religion and Logic

From what has been said above (Section 6) it follows that we must first examine the problem of the existence or—what is the same—of the legitimacy of a LR. This study will comprehend three parts.

In the first part, we shall state the problem in general. Here, after a historical survey (Section 7), we shall formulate the questions to be answered (Section 8).

The second part will be devoted to these problems which are relevant to RD. After clarifying some aspects of the concept of meaning basic to RD (Section 9), we shall enumerate the different types of theories of religion which appear as *a priori* possible in the framework of what has been said about meaning (Section 10). Then three theories, which are of greater relevance to our subject, will be selected for closer examination: the nonsense theory or the theory of the Unspeakable (Section 11), the non-communicativist theory

(Section 12), and the theory according to which no propositions are intended to be communicated by any parts of the RD (Section 13).

In the third part, the necessary conditions for a LR will be studied from the viewpoint of logic. We shall ask ourselves therefore if the claim of the universality of formal logic (Section 14) and of general semantics (Section 15) is justified. A final paragraph will be devoted to the so-called dialectical logic or dialectics, which is sometimes said to be the proper LR (Section 16).

7.   On the history of the relations between logic and religion

One striking fact in the history of religion is the coexistence inside the religious communities of two radically opposed trends as to the relations which exist between religion and logic. We shall call them "the anti-logical trend" and "the logical trend."

1. There have been—it seems—in all religions, many prominent thinkers who have categorically denied any applicability of logic to religion. Moreover, some among them considered logic as something which by its very nature is contrary to religion. Thus Peter Damian said that logic is the work of the Devil and this evaluation, taken over by Luther, is sometimes proposed even today. There is an abundant religious literature in all religions which advises the believer not to reason, but to pray and worship, and there are some sectors of

religious communities which are quite opposed to any logic. This is a well-established historical fact.

2. However, the presence of the logical trend is also a well-established fact. Every great religion seems to have had some periods where the application of logic to religion was considered as something quite natural and legitimate. Such has been the case of Islam at least since the ninth century, of Christianity during the thirteenth to the fifteenth centuries, of Buddhism between the sixth and eighth centuries in India, of Brahmanism at the time of the Vedanta (since the ninth century) and even earlier (Nyāya). During such periods, not only is the existing logic thoroughly applied to religion insofar as rational theology or Buddhology is built up, but there is even much creative work in pure logic by religious thinkers.

It might be said, of course, and as a matter of fact it has been said often enough, that these periods were times of religious decadence, that thinkers who did apply logic to religion were really not religious thinkers at all. In the face of such assertions, we are bound to ask: What is the criterion of a truly religious thinker? It seems that 7.1   at least one such criterion is available: we may legitimately call "religion"—"true religion"—that which was practiced by men and women who are universally considered to be saints or saintly believers of their respective religions.

But when we apply this criterion, it appears that

there have been not a few saints and saintly persons in history who were at the same time good logicians and did apply logic to their religion. One instance is Dignāna, a saintly Mahayana mystic, who was a leading and creative Hindu logician. Another is St. Albert the Great, who was able to write, on the one hand, deeply religious books about the Mother of God (in which, incidentally, he asks *utrum novit logicam?*), and, on the other, most subtle treatises of formal logic. A third, little-known instance is Savonarola, a saintly preacher, who was also a powerful thinker in logic and dealt with the problems of antinomies with great penetration.

It follows that we have no right, as historians, to classify the logical trend as not being truly
7.2   religious. The situation we are faced with is that there are two trends in history of religion: the anti-logical and the logical.

As far as the anti-logical trend is concerned, it is easy to understand the causes of its existence: on one side, the radical difference between the attitudes of a believer and those of a logician as such; on the other, the fact that many adversaries of the religions in question did use their logic in order to combat religion.

But it is equally easy to see why so many—often very prominent—representatives of different religions were partisans of the logical trend.

The basic reason is the belief common to most of the great religions that the world is ruled by logical laws—that God acts according to geometrical laws, or that everything happens according to the Karma, and so on. This belief must have prompted the believers of these religions to consider logic itself as something positive and worthy of enquiry.

Secondary reasons seem to have been, on one side, the (paradoxically) rationalist character of religious beliefs, founded on the certainty given to the believers by their faith that there are no inconsistencies between their Creed and the results of reasoning. The stronger the faith was, the stronger that belief must have been. On the other hand, many among the religions see reason as the properly divine element in man and consider its cultivation as a religious duty.

This explains why the presence of both tendencies is, so to say, quite natural and to be expected, even if it were not so well substantiated by what we know from history.

8. The problem of a logic of religion

Although there is no difficulty in applying logic to science, the possibility of applying it to religion is problematic and has been often denied, as we have seen in the preceding section.

The main considerations which may be formulated against such a possibility are the following:

1. Religion is obviously a field of human activities in which emotions predominate; logic, on the contrary, is known as the paramount case of purely

rational activity. There seems, therefore, to be radical opposition between the two fields.

2. Religion is a subjective affair: it is "what man does with his solitude" (Whitehead). But logic is rightly considered as embodying the summit of objectivity; it is, consequently, a quite impersonal activity. For this reason also there seems to be no possible application of logic to religion.

3. Finally, even if there are propositions in religion, these propositions are accepted on faith; the basic attitude of a believer as such is that of trust. Logic, on the contrary, is based exclusively on scientific insight and rigorous proof. Insofar as logic is concerned, it has been rightly said to be "the moral of proof," as it supplies the highest standards of exactness in demonstration. We have, consequently, to do with two radically opposed attitudes and it is hard to see how logic could be applied to religion.

These arguments look formidable indeed; and as a matter of fact they convincingly show at least one thing: that religious activity and logical activity are not identical. They are even so much opposed that it is hard to conceive of a man who could perform a religious act and an act of logic at the same time. So much must be, therefore, granted.

But this is not all. Religious activity is not only distinct from logical activity, but it also does not need any logic, whereas science does in its own field. A believer performs an act of faith, of trust, of worship, and so on, and all this does not need any demonstration in order to be carried out. A logical analysis introduced into an act of prayer would most probably damage if not destroy this act as such.

But with regard to logical analysis, the situation which arises in religion may be compared with that which we observe in an act of love. This too is not a scientific act, has quite different characteristics, and does not need any science to be carried on. The lover does not need to know anything about hormones or complexes in order to love. Yet a science of love is possible and does, as a matter of fact, exist. So too a science—or rather a number of sciences—of religion exists: religious psychology, sociology, and so on. These sciences share with logic its rational, objective, and social character. If such other sciences of religion are legitimate and possible, why should logic of religion be impossible, one may ask? The difference in objectivity, rationality, and so on, between logic and these other sciences is not an essential one—at most it is a difference of degree.

If we consider the situation from this angle, it appears that none of the arguments quoted above do force the conclusion that no logic of religion is possible. They only prove that logic of religion is different from religion itself—but this is granted by everybody.

It is true that, in order to demonstrate the existence of a logic of religion, more conditions must be fulfilled than is the case in demonstrating, for example, the existence of psychology of religion; rather, the conditions are quite different. These conditions must be discussed in detail and will be so later on. But nothing in the general argumentation sketched here prevents the *a priori* possibility of such a discipline.

9. On meaning

In order to be able to discuss the various theories about the legitimacy of LR, we must start with a sketch of the different sorts of meaning which may be carried by discourse and, consequently, by RD. This tabulation is taken essentially from the old Stoic school; it appears to be more complete than the divisions now in use. In one point it had to be completed for our present purposes.

The division is as follows:

An utterance may be either meaningless or meaningful. If it is meaningful, it may have either a purely subjective (that is, relaxative) meaning or an objective meaning. In both cases—but only the objective is of interest here—it may be communicative or non-communicative; as an example of the non-communicative we may think of a sort of shorthand one uses for himself only, and which nobody else can read. Communicative objective meaning is either complete or incomplete. A complete meaning is one carried by an utterance or other symbol which may be meaningfully stated alone, without being a part of a larger formula. Complete meanings are propositions, performatives, imperatives, prayers, and so on. Incomplete meanings are such structures as those expressed by predicates, subjects and, perhaps, by many other sorts of symbols.

$$\text{Meaning} \begin{cases} \text{objective} \\ \text{subjective} \end{cases} \begin{cases} \text{communicative} \\ \text{non-communicative} \end{cases} \begin{cases} \text{complete} \\ \text{incomplete} \end{cases} \begin{cases} \text{propositions} \\ \text{others} \end{cases}$$

This is one system of division of meaning. There is also another, independent of it which, after being a standard part of Scholastic semantics and despite its importance, has been practically forgotten: a symbol may have meaning either by convention or by its material nature (*signum instrumentale* and *signum naturale*). The most important case of the latter is the image (*signum formale*). One instance of such *signa formalia* is a fugue of Bach. This presents and, consequently, communicates a highly complex objective structure, but does not do it by convention, as words do: it "shows" it, to use Wittgenstein's famous words. A *signum formale* is always communicative but it seems that, by its very nature, it always communicates something incomplete, not a proposition or a similar complete structure.

A remark about the poverty of most semantic analyses of the present day is in order here. It is all too often said that every meaning is either theoretical or emotional; and by "theoretical," propositional meaning is meant. By this (1) all non-propositional complete meanings, such as those of performatives, imperatives, and so on, are reduced to the status of purely emotional meanings, which is simply preposterous; (2) such meanings as those carried by music are also declared to be purely emotional, which is—if this is possible—more preposterous still. The reason for this poverty is, however, clear: most semanticians are exclusively interested in science. Science is, however, composed of propositions; it is, consequently, sufficient to divide all meaning into propositional and "other." Yet there is no justification for calling all the "other" meanings "emotional," as is so often done—because this does not fit the real situation. There is many a meaning which is not propositional and yet not emotive at all.

We may also note that a symbol having objective meaning, such as a sentence, may also have, at the same time, emotional meaning. Indeed, this is usually the case. In RD there is probably not a single symbol which does not carry some emotional meaning. But the question which we have to dis-cuss asks if it carries *only* such emotional meaning or whether, perhaps, it also carries some other meaning and, if so, what sort of meaning?

10.   Theories of religion
The table of meanings above supplies a guide to the theories of religion which are *a priori* possible. They are the following:

1. Nonsense theory. RD has no meaning at all.

2. Emotionalist theory. The meaning of RD is purely emotional, that is, relaxative. This doctrine is sometimes ascribed to Schleiermacher.

3. Non-communicativist theory. RD does indeed have objective meaning, but this is not communicable.

4. Communicativist, non-propositional theories. Here RD has some objective, communicative meaning but this meaning is not propositional. One outstanding type of such theories is the doctrine according to which RD means, in its communicative parts, rules of action. When we read in a religious text, for example, that God is good, the meaning is that man should be good to his neighbors, and so on.

5. Theory of incomplete meanings. This theory, which does not seem to have been explicitly proposed in history, would assert that all objective communicative meaning in RD is incomplete.

6. Propositional theory. At least some parts of RD are intended to mean propositions.

It may be remarked that, from the point of view of the theory n, whatever is said by the theories preceding n in our table is true for some parts of RD; the theory n asserts, however, that other parts of RD have also another sort of meaning.

For example, from the point of view of the propositional theory (the strongest semantically), there may be some parts of RD which express rules, incomplete meanings, non-communicative objective meanings, and, above all, emotions; moreover, it may be admitted from the point of view of such a theory, that some parts of RD do not have any meaning at all, but are uttered for other purposes. This may be the case, for example, of "*Om mani padme hum*" which, if meaningful in itself, is not used as such in prayers, but rather as a sort of stimulus. Therefore, these theories are named in the above table in order of increasing strength.

What will be the fate of logic of religion on the basis of each of these theories?

1. If all RD is nonsense, there will be no LR at all.

2. Only semantics of RD will be possible on the basis of the emotionalist theory.

3. No LR at all will be possible on the basis of the non-communicativist theory. For logic is essentially concerned with meaningful terms; and logic is a science, that is, it is intersubjective. But according to this theory RD is not intersubjectively meaningful.

4. According to the theory of incomplete meaning, both semantics and formal logic of RD are possible. Formal logic of RD will be difficult to establish because all the formal logic we have is exclusively concerned with propositions. However, the *a priori* possibility is present.

5. If meaning of RD is objective, communicative, and complete, but non-propositional, then semantics, formal logic, and perhaps some sort of methodology are possible. Here again, except in the case

of the rules of action, we have very few logical tools but the task is *a priori* possible.

6. Finally, on the basis of the propositional theory a full logic of religion will be possible, comprehending all three parts of logic. Moreover, as the logic of propositions (not to be confounded with propositional logic alone!) is a well-developed science, the task will be much easier on the basis of this theory than on the basis of the other theories.

From the logical point of view, the following questions are, therefore, of fundamental importance: is RD intended by its user to have:

1. Communicative objective meaning?
2. Propositional meaning?

These questions have to be answered before any enquiry in the LR may be undertaken. It must be noted, however, that even if they are both answered in an affirmative way LR will not be exempt from the study of such aspects of RD which are not only allowed by the theories 2–5, but also allowed by the propositional theory. For this statement does not deny that, as was said above, there are, in addition to the propositional, also other meanings in RD.

11. On the Unspeakable

The first problem to be considered is whether there is meaning at all in religious discourse. The view that there is none has been often expressed when the respective authors were saying that the object of religion (abbreviated here as "OR") is unspeakable. We shall call such a doctrine "the theory of the Unspeakable."

This theory has often enough been said to be inconsistent, the argument in favor of this contention being roughly the following: the theory states that nothing can be said about the OR, but it does itself say something about it; consequently, it entails a contradiction. And, if so, the theory must be obviously rejected.

The situation is, however, more complex than this. It will be argued here that the theory of the Unspeakable:

1. Does not entail an obvious contradiction.

2. Yet it does not fit the needs of RD.

11.1 *I. The theory of the Unspeakable is not inconsistent.* It is asserted that, if the conventions usually accepted in logic are adhered to, no immediate inconsistency appears in the theory under consideration. If in a certain frame of reference this theory leads to contradictions this must be shown by those who assert that this is so; but such proof has not been given as yet, as far as is known to this author. On the contrary, it is easy to show that there does not need to be an inconsistency in the theory.

Let us write "$Un(x, y)$" for "x is an unspeakable object in the language y," and let us consider, first, the formula:

(1) $$(\exists\, x,\, l)Un(x,\, l).$$

Can it be asserted without inconsistency? Of course it can; moreover, it is obviously true. For it is very easy to find an object x and a language l which satisfy $Un(x, l)$.

But if this is so, by elementary laws of logic formula (1) is true. One instance is the cow and the language of chess; it is quite obvious that the cow is unspeakable in the language of chess, that is, that nothing can be said about it in that language. And there is no inconsistency — it seems — in it.

Let us now universalize and consider the formula

$$(2) \qquad\qquad (l)Un(o, l),$$

where "o" is a constant. This seems to be a far more serious matter, namely, here it is asserted that o is unspeakable in any language, which seems to lead to a contradiction. However, it can be shown that this is not so if we apply the usual conventions established in order to avoid semantic antinomies. In the present state of research it is safe to admit that no formula in which something is said about a class of languages can be formulated in any of these languages; in other words, in order to be meaningful the statement itself must be formulated in another language, which is the corresponding meta-language.

For our purpose, where o is OR it is best to consider the class of all languages referred to in (2) as the class of object languages; then (2) is stated in the first-grade meta-language. It is then meaning-ful and in no way inconsistent. For exactly as in the case of formula (1) it is not inconsistent to state in one language that *o* is unspeakable in another language or in an element of a class of languages, provided that the language in which the statement is made does not belong to that class.

But if this is so, the theory of the Unspeakable does not entail any obvious inconsistency. No serious objection can be formulated against it from the standpoint of general logic.

11.2   *II. The theory of the Unspeakable is not satisfactory for RD.* However, the situation changes if we consider this theory from the point of view of applied logic which is, in our case, the logic of RD. It may be legitimately asked whether, in the frame of ref-erence of the RD, (2) does not entail some contra-dictions. It is contended here that it does.

Let us consider, first, what the consequences of (2) are. If the above hypothesis is accepted, that is, if we consider the class of languages referred to in (2) as being the class of all object-languages, or as containing that class, then it appears that (2) ex-cludes the attribution to OR of any object-linguistic property at all. The only property which can be at-tributed to it is, by (2), the meta-linguistic prop-erty of being unspeakable in any of those lan-guages. Moreover, it seems that, according to the theory of the Unspeakable, the formula

$$(\exists x)(l)Un(x, l)$$

describes OR and that there is, according to it, no other description of OR. This means, however, that the believer who, as such, accepts only such propositions as are expressed in some RD does not accept and cannot accept any proposition ascribing to the OR any object-linguistic property. All that he accepts about it is that it is unspeakable. It is this consequence which is inconsistent with actual RD. This appears directly as far as the propositional element of the RD is concerned, and indirectly in regard to the non-propositional element.

1. The propositional element. Every religious discourse contains at least some sentences which purport to ascribe to OR (a) object-linguistic properties, (b) several such properties.

a. At least some object-linguistic properties are ascribed to OR. For example, in Christian religion it is said that God is the creator of the world. It seems sheerly impossible to interpret this statement as meaning only that nothing can be said about God. On the contrary, it seems obvious that some relation to the world — whatever it might be — has been asserted here. And such a relation is an object-linguistic, not a meta-linguistic, property.

b. Moreover, several different properties of this sort seem to be always ascribed to the OR. To quote another instance, it is said in the Catholic Creed that God created the world and that God is one in three Persons. Again it seems quite impossible to conceive that both properties are exactly the same.

It follows that there is a class, a non-empty class, and even a class containing more than one element, of object-linguistic properties ascribed to OR in RD.

2. The non-propositional element. Here object-linguistic properties are clearly assumed. Let us consider, for example, that subclass of utterances in RD elements of which are phrases of praise, worship, and so on. They all suppose that the user of such phrases assumes their object — that is, OR — to possess some high value. Now value can be attributed to an object only under the condition that at least one factual object-linguistic property has been assumed as belonging to it. It seems a sheer impossibility to worship, that is, to value, an entity about which one is prepared to assume only that it cannot be spoken about. Such an entity is, for the user, completely void of any object-linguistic property. It could be, for example, the Devil. There is absolutely no reason why it should be worshiped, praised, and so on.

The theory of the Unspeakable must, therefore, be discarded.

12. On communicativeness in RD

We shall now examine the claim of the non-communicativist theory, according to which no part of RD, except perhaps such as carries purely emotional meaning, is communicative. The terms of RD do mean something objective on the basis of this theory; but that something cannot be communicated, that is, made known to others by the users of RD.

That such situations may arise is, indeed, easy to understand. We may think, for example, of a prisoner, who, in order to fix his memory, or to enjoy some remembrances, talks "to himself" in his cell in a language which none of his coprisoners understands. In that case his utterances have meaning, but only for the user, not for those who hear them. If examination of the non-communicative meaning is seldom made, this is perhaps due to the fact that we too often consider meaning as a purely semantical concept, whereas it is really a pragmatic one. In the frame of reference of pragmatics it is, of course, clear that a sign-vehicle s has some meaning m for some person p; if we write "$U(x, y, z)$" for "x uses the term y in the meaning z" and "$M(y, z, x)$" for "the term y means z for the person x," then we can formulate the above state of affairs as follows in regard to a class of utterances α:

$$(y): \cdot y \in \alpha \cdot \supset \cdot (x, y) \cdot U(x, y, z) \supset \cdot (t) \cdot M(y, z, t) \supset t = x.$$

This is what is claimed by the non-communicativist theory about RD.

There are two different possible interpretations of this claim.

a. The radical interpretation. Given any two persons, say a and b, when a uses RD, b does not understand what a means, and reciprocally, when b uses it, a does not understand the utterances of b. RD is completely meaningless to the receiver even though it is meaningful to the user.

If the theory is interpreted in this way, it is obviously wrong. This can be shown in the following way. Whenever two or more persons use the same utterances and react to them in similar ways, that is, behave similarly when hearing or reading them, there is at least a very high probability that they both understand them in the same way. But two or more believers of the same religion — in fact, roughly speaking all of them — use the same RD and react similarly to it. Therefore, there is at least a high probability that they understand it in a similar way, which is against the theory. This argues, then, that it is an established fact that no believer understands any part of RD when RD is uttered by another believer. But there is nothing to support this in empirical evidence, and everything we know about the behavior of believers contradicts it. The non-communicativist theory must be, therefore, discarded in this interpretation.

b. The occasionalist interpretation. This is a more subtle version of the same theory. It does not deny that two or more persons do attach to the same elements of RD the same meaning. However, it contends that the meaning has not been communicated by one believer to another, but has been obtained by the second believer independently of RD. The first believer is, then, just the occasional cause of the understanding. To use a comparison, it is as if the hearing of a piece of music prompted somebody to understand the meaning of a mathematical formula he was thinking about.

The partisans of this theory contend, moreover, that the meaning attached by the receiver to the utterances is directly infused by a supernatural agency and, so to say, created in his mind. There is a common meaning attached to the terms of RD, but there is no communication.

This theory is certainly not logically inconsistent. The question is, however, not its logical consistency but rather its consistency with what we know about the behavior of the users and receivers of RD; it may also be asked what the use of such a hypothesis is. The answer in both cases is unfavorable to the theory.

1. It is not excluded that some parts of RD are not intended to communicate an objective meaning, but rather to act as stimuli which may help evoke some experiences (mostly emotional ones) by the receivers. But when we consider the bulk of RD, above all its central parts, namely, Scriptures, Creeds, and so on, we find that the authors of such parts of RD do quite obviously intend to communicate something by the terms they use and that they do, moreover, succeed in doing so. This is, perhaps, most obvious in those parts of RD which contain commandments; but it is also clearly present in many other parts of RD. The fact that such authors, and also all preachers and teachers of

religion, go to great lengths in order to make themselves understood by their hearers and readers also points in the same direction. To be brief, although nothing supports the occasionalist theory in its generality, most of what we know about RD contradicts it.

2. The theory supposes a sort of continuous miracle operated by the supernatural agency. This must occur every time a believer perceives a text belonging to the RD. Now such a continuous miracle is certainly logically possible — but in face of the fact that the situation may be explained in a far simpler way by supposing that RD is communicative, it is hardly probable that it occurs.

12.1   Therefore, the non-communicativist theory must be discarded on empirical grounds even in its weaker, occasionalist, interpretation.

13.   On religious propositions

The third problem with which we are concerned here is that of the religious propositions. It may be formulated in the following terms: are some parts of RD intended by their users to mean propositions? This is denied by the partisans of all theories of religion other than that which we called "propositional theory." They contend that no part of RD is ever intended to mean propositions. It may express feelings, mean rules of action, represent some other complete structures, like prayers, and so on, but it is never intended to mean propositions.

The problem is an empirical one. We are not asking whether it is logically correct to assert that there are religious propositions; we are trying to see whether believers do think that they are dealing with and asserting propositions.

As in the previous cases, nobody denies that there are vast parts of RD which are not intended to mean propositions — for example, all those parts which express prayers and so on. But the question is whether this is true of all parts of RD, whether there is no single part of it which is propositional. So formulated, the question must be answered by the following theorem:

13.1   *Some parts of the RD of every religion are intended by their users to express and assert propositions.*

The proof is as follows. We see that many parts of RD have the grammatical form of indicative sentences, which normally are used to express propositions. Many among them, especially those which are parts of the Creed, are said to be believed by the respective believers. Now, it is true that the term "believe" may be interpreted in such a way that it is not necessary to admit that whatever one believes is a proposition. But the following test precludes all possibilities of doubt about the character of belief as used in RD. First, we ask a believer of *r* if he believes a sentence *P*, which is part of the RD of *r*. He, of course, will say that he does. Then we ask him if he thinks that *P* is true. It seems that there can be no doubt about the answer: the be-

liever will always answer that he does, that he thinks
P to be true. But a formula can be true only if it
means a proposition. Therefore, the believers think
that some parts of RD express propositions. Therefore the theorem is true.

We suffer, as has already been stressed, under
the handicap of not having at hand any serious
empirical enquiries into the factual behavior of believers. However, neither do our adversaries have
any such help and, moreover, whatever we know
about the behavior of believers points quite clearly
to the propositional character of some parts of their
religious discourse. The evidence in favor of this
thesis has not, it is true, been systematically elaborated, but it is still overwhelming.

In the face of this evidence, it must be stated that
theoreticians who assert that there is no propositional element at all in RD do not offer any analysis
of the factually existing RD, but rather are sug-
gesting a completely new sort of RD. To put this
quite bluntly, they are advising believers to cease
being believers. Because "believer" has meant up to
now — and still means — simply a man who believes
some propositions and ascribes to them a truth-
value.

14.   On the universality of logic
In the foregoing sections the basic conditions,
necessary in order that a full LR be possible, have
been shown to be present: there is in religion a dis-

course which is (1) meaningful, (2) communicative, and (3) partly, at least, propositional. It follows that, if logic applies to every discourse which is meaningful, communicative, and expresses propositions, it also applies to RD.

However, this hypothesis has been denied by many writers, who contended that "religion lies beyond the limits of logic." By this, two different propositions seem to be meant. Sometimes the proposition that formal logic does not apply to the RD is meant; in other cases, authors who use this phrase mean that semantics do not have any legitimate application to it.

We shall first examine the first proposition. It has often been said that one characteristic of RD is its "paradoxical" character or, in proper terms, its inconsistency.* For example, it has been said that Christian RD contains the (atomic) sentence "Christ is God," which entails a contradiction, and the (molecular) sentence "The Father is God, the Son is God, but the Father is not the Son," which is inconsistent in itself. The examples chosen are strikingly naive, because one obviously supposes that such terms as "is" always have—in any axiomatic context—the same "natural" meaning, ignoring the fact that they may have different meanings and different syntactical properties in RD and outside it. But examples are rather irrelevant. As this

---

*"Paradoxical" sometimes also has a weaker meaning; we are, however, not concerned with this weaker meaning here.

theory—we shall call it the "a-logical theory"—has been defended by so many writers, it is necessary to discuss it briefly.

Some of the partisans of the a-logical theory may have been prompted to sustain it because they really did believe that RD is either non-communicative or, if communicative, has a purely emotional meaning. If so, they have expressed themselves incorrectly, since such discourse is neither consistent nor inconsistent (only propositional discourse can be such). This position is, consequently, not relevant to our present problem.

Most of the partisans of the a-logical theory seem to take RD to be communicative and propositional; yet they contend that it "lies beyond the limits of logic," that is, that it is inconsistent. In this they join a vast class of philosophers who preach the same theory in regard to many other fields. Such writers are really skeptics as to logic, and it is a well-known fact that no argument is really effective against a skeptic. There is no use, in particular, in trying to convince him about the nature of formal logic.

There is, however, one ground on which he can be met: on the condition that he admits the communicative and propositional character of RD or of its parts. For then the a-logical theory may be refuted in the following way.

A communicative sentence is one which communicates something; this is the definition of communicativity. But in order to communicate something, a selection must be made by the symbol in the range of possibilities given. Consequently, every communicative symbol indicates such a selection. For example, when somebody says that this cow is black, he selects, among the many colors which the cow may be, one only and asserts it of the cow. But an inconsistent symbol does not indicate any selection at all. For example, when somebody says that this cow is both black and non-black, he has not indicated any selection, since the non-black contains all other colors. His statement is, therefore, void and, as such, does not communicate anything. It follows that an inconsistent symbol is not communicative, which is against the assumption made by the partisans of the theory.

And if they object that we are using logic to show this—whereas they reject logic—the answer is that we are using logic not in the field of RD but in quite general discourse. Also the amount of logic used in the above reasoning is very, very small—the reasoning itself only makes clear a quite obvious proposition: that whoever talks inconsistently does not say anything.

Therefore, the a-logical theory must be discarded.

14.1 And as a consequence, it must be said that formal logic does apply to RD.

15. On the universality of semantics

As corollary to the doctrine of the non-applicability of formal logic to RD, it is often said that semantics does not apply to it either. For, it is contended, semantics is a theory of human language; whereas RD is not a human language, it is a divine language.

Now there are several ways of interpreting this last statement. For one thing, RD is about things Divine, or at least transcendent; this fact offers, of course, serious semantic difficulties. But these difficulties all arise in the frame of reference of the usual semantic laws, and it is not easy to see why the fact that a language is about a particular object should prevent its being a language, that is, subject to the same laws.

Another way in which the sentence can be understood is this: RD is the language of God or of another transcendent agent. This, again, is quite legitimate if a given Creed is assumed as true. But, again, it does not follow that the language used by this agent must, or even can, be different in principle from the usual human language.

In other words, what is contended here is that RD may be divine insofar as it is about God and divine in as far as it is used by God, but that it still remains a human language insofar as its formal nature is concerned. To use Aristotelian terminology, RD is divine materially and causally, but remains human formally: materially, because God is its subject matter; causally, because He is the agent using it; but not formally, as its structure is human.

That this is so, that no RD can be divine in the

last meaning of the word (formally), can be seen in the following way.

Suppose that a supernatural agent, say G, wishes to communicate to a human being H, some proposition. G, who is supposed to be omnipotent or at least very potent, may have at his disposal means of communicating this proposition directly, without using any discourse, without any symbols at all. If so, there is no RD and consequently no problem at all. However, in all religions with which we are concerned it is assumed that G did decide to use some symbols, and even a quite elaborate discourse to communicate to men what he wanted to tell them. Buddha, Christ, and other founders of religions always did so; and in every religion there are a number of statements of that sort which make up a considerable portion of the propositional sector of its RD.

Now if this is so, whatever the power of the supernatural might be, he is still subject to the most general laws of logic, which, applied to the given situation, give rise to the following state of affairs:

1. G wishes to communicate to H the proposition p.

2. Therefore, he associates an utterance, say P to p, and makes H perceive P.

3. H perceives P materially, as a mere phenomenon (for example, as a noise, or as a heap of dry ink on paper).

4. H then deciphers P by associating to it p.

Now, all this is a normal semiotical situation arising whenever the user of a discourse wishes thereby to communicate something to a receiver of the same. And there is no other way for this user — whoever he may be — to communicate anything to the receiver if he wishes to use symbols. But as has already been said, use of symbols is the case in every religion considered here. Therefore, we must find the same general semiotic situation in RD as elsewhere.

But if this is so, there is no way of conceiving the RD as lying beyond semantics. For the above-described semiotic situation is ruled, among others, by the laws of semantics. And this is so because semantics is nothing else but logical analysis of the given situation — its laws are not empirical generalizations, but logically true laws. And outside of logic there is nothing but nonsense. We have seen, however, that the nonsense theory of RD cannot be accepted.

15.1 Therefore, it is not true that RD is beyond semantics. It lies, on the contrary, completely within semantics and is subject to its laws as is every other discourse.

16. On dialectics and its use in logic of religion

The most radical objections against what has been said above are usually formulated by the partisans of the so-called dialectics, or dialectical logic; consequently, a few words should be said about this logic.

When analyzing the writings, mostly very confused, of these authors—called "dialecticians" here —we usually find that the term "dialectics" and the expression "dialectical logic" do not have one single meaning but several meanings. In other words, dialectics is dialectical itself. The following meanings may be distinguished:

1. *The purely methodological meaning.* Used in this way, "dialectics" means a method which consists of some rules of operating with concepts during the period preceding formalization. We should then, it is said, see the objects in their context, consider the tendencies to which they are subjected, see the oppositions existing between them, study the diversity of aspects of everything, and so on. As far as this is concerned, dialectics or dialectical logic is nothing other than a number of suggestions on how to observe, and so on, before formalizing. One would be tempted to say that, as such, dialectics partially coincides with what is often called the "phenomenological method," and other elements of it remind us of certain elements of the methodology of deductive sciences, among others the theory of axiomatic systems. There seems to be nothing to object to in such suggestions. Indeed, the stressing of the need for such operations before reasoning and especially before formalization is begun could be very important. For only a subject matter which has already been sufficiently digested by pre-formal analysis is suitable for formal operations, and many mistakes have resulted from too

much haste in applying formal reasoning before having sufficiently prepared the subject matter.

2. *The psychological meaning.* So understood, "dialectics" asserts that the mind is constituted in such a way that it cannot work with fixed meanings, with well-determined concepts, and if it does so occasionally, then it simplifies these concepts to the extent that they lose any real importance. This, it must be clearly said, is simply untrue. Whatever may be the facts about reality, the mind is certainly constituted in a way exactly opposed to what the dialecticians say, namely, it can operate exclusively with fixed concepts. It can, of course, change the meaning of the terms, that is, the concepts, but it always passes from one determined concept to another determined concept and does not seem to be able to work with anything else.

3. *The ontological meaning.* When used in this way, "dialectics" refers to a doctrine according to which this same indeterminacy is found in reality. There are no determined objects in reality, because everything is subjected to constant change. Therefore, nothing quite determined can be said of anything; for example, one cannot say that a body *a* is in a certain place *l*, because it always moves and, consequently, is and is not in *l* at the same time and under the same conditions. This ontological theory, although assuming a true premiss, draws from it wrong consequences. The true premiss is that every real thing and property is al-

ways changing. But it does not follow that every-thing is indeterminate. In order to see this, it is enough to consider that the expression "to be" does not need to mean "to stay without motion in one place." We may quite legitimately use it as meaning "to move from A to B during the time interval t." It is also enough, to refute the conclusion of inde-terminacy, to conceive of l not as a mathematical point but as an interval. If we do so, it will appear that the whole ontological dialectics is the result of a rather trivial linguistic misunderstanding.

4. The semantic meaning. Finally, "dialectics" may refer to a semantic theory according to which no word has a fixed meaning. Some authors used to say even more; they seemed to say that the very meanings themselves are subject to the same "law" of indeterminacy which is said to apply to reality. This view is surely contradicted by everything we know about meanings, and what has been said about the psychological meaning of "dialectics" also applies here. There is nothing more deter-minate than most of our meanings, and, indeed, it is hard to understand how we could think and com-municate our thoughts if it were not so.

16.1　So much for dialectics in general. As applied to RD, there seems to be only one fruitful way of using it—namely, by understanding it to be a set of sugges-tions about the analysis of RD before we proceed to any formalization. All other uses of dialectic can-not have any point at all.

III

The Structure of Religious Discourse

In this chapter purely structural problems of RD will be discussed, with the supposition that all questions of meaning and of justification are provisionally solved.

We shall proceed as follows. It will be necessary, first of all, to clarify some basic points about the structure of the discourse in general (Section 17); then the general structural problems of RD will be stated (Section 18); we shall then examine the structure of RD (Section 19), its explicit axiomatization (Section 20), and a syntactical problem, namely, the syntactic structure of "God" (Section 21). Next the relations between π and ρ will be studied, first in general (Section 22), then especially in regard to $\pi \cap \rho$ and $-\pi \cap -\rho$, where the concept of $\tau'\rho$ will be introduced (Section 24). A paragraph will be then devoted to the formal logic of $\tau'\rho$ (Section 25) and two to TD (total discourse), in which its structure (Section 26) and inconsistencies (Section 27) will be considered. A last paragraph will treat of para-religious discourse (Section 28).

17. On the formal structure
of a discourse and its problems

Every propositional discourse (which is, *a fortiori*, a meaningful discourse) is structured in some way. It need not be—and often is not—axiomatized, that is, its different factors are not explicitly stated; but, nevertheless, some structure is always present. If this is often overlooked, it is because we are so accustomed to applying its rules that we do not notice them.

The types of discourse most studied up to now are our modern axiomatic systems. In such a system we usually find the following elements:

1. A class of meta-linguistic rules, indicating which expressions are expressions of the system.

2. A meta-linguistic rule indicating which sentences are to be assumed as valid in the system without proof.

3. A class of meta-linguistic rules indicating how, from a sentence valid in the system, other sentences valid in it can be derived.

4. A class of object-linguistic expressions which, having the characteristics indicated by (1), are well-formed expressions of the system.

5. A class of object-linguistic sentences which, having the characteristics indicated by (2), are the axioms of the system.

6. A class of sentences which, having been derived, directly or indirectly, from the axioms (4) by the use of the rules (3) are valid (derived) theorems of the system.

This is the ideal case of a formalized axiomatic system; such types of discourse are rare and it is doubtful if there are many outside pure logic. Nevertheless, the study of such an axiomatized system allows one to see what the structure of each discourse must be. For even if the structure is neither formalized nor even intuitively axiomatized, as is the case in most sciences, it must have at least one characteristic in common with the formalized systems, namely, there must be a distinction in it between a class of object-linguistic expressions and a class of meta-linguistic rules indicating what expressions are meaningful and, in the case of sentences, which are valid in the system.

For our purposes it will be necessary to examine briefly only that part of the above structure which is concerned with sentences. According to what has been said, this consists of a class of meta-linguistic rules indicating which sentences are to be recognized as valid in the system, and of a class of such valid object-linguistic sentences, whether they are axioms or derived theorems.

However, when a system is not studied exclusively for its internal structure—as it is with logicians—that is, when its theorems are recognized (with some interpretation) by a subject as valid, then a third factor is needed, namely, a rule stating that any sentence belonging to the class of axioms or derived theorems of the system is to be accepted as valid. Then we have three factors:

1. The class of valid sentences; this is object-linguistic; it consists, in the case of an axiomatized system, of axioms and derived theorems. It will be called here "objective content."

2. The class of rules determining which sentences belong to the objective content. These rules —which are meta-linguistic—will be called "heuristic rules."

3. The meta-linguistic statement that every sentence designated by the heuristic rule is valid. This statement will be called here the "basic assumption."

Another remark must be added. The objective content of a discourse is usually itself structured, insofar as some of its elements are assumed as axioms and others are derived from them. However, once a certain number of such derived sentences has been obtained, a reorganization of the objective content is often carried out; and now some of the sentences which have been derived are taken as axioms, whereas others—and among them the very axioms of the primitive system—are deduced and become proved theorems.

This may be best seen in the field of physics or of any other sufficiently developed natural science. Here we have, first, a set of axioms designated by the heuristic rule under the basic assumption. These axioms are, obviously, the experimental sentences, that is, the sentences expressing propositions about observed facts. From these sentences, with the use of some previously established theorems and of certain rules of (inductive) derivation, explanatory sentences such as general laws, hypotheses, and so on are obtained. The explanatory sentences are again explained in a similar way by more general sentences. At a given point in time, the mass of sentences making up the objective content of physics is reorganized in such a way that now one or more among the explanatory sentences is taken as an axiom and the remaining sentences are derived from them by means of the rules of deductive logic. An important point is that here the very sentences which played the role of axioms in the primitive system now become derived theorems.

We have, consequently, in every such field a twofold virtual axiomatization. In the first axiomatization, only experimental sentences (along with some mathematical laws) are axioms; in the second, on the contrary, these sentences are derived theorems, whereas some sentences which were derived in the first system are now axioms.

This distinction is often overlooked, especially by those who consider mathematics of a Platonic type as being the paradigm of every axiomatization. In mathematics of this type these two sets of axioms coincide—and this because all rules used are deductive. But in the empirical sciences a distinction must be drawn in order to avoid misunderstanding.

We shall term the axioms of the first systems—namely, those obtained by means of the heuristic rules—"basic sentences" or alternatively "epistemic axioms"; the axioms of the second system will be called "logical axioms." The expression "logical axioms" is somewhat inadequate, but it will do here for practical reasons.

The main structural problems of a discourse may now be enumerated in the following way:

First, there will be a class of quite generic problems, concerned with the first systems, that is, with the nature of the basic assumption, of the heuristic rules, and of the objective content of the discourse.

Then problems will arise as to the logical structure of the objective content itself, in particular as to the formal logic used in its second axiomatization. It is a well-known fact that, for example, in microphysics, some sort of many-valued logic seems to be necessary.

Third, a number of questions may sometimes arise as to the relations between a given discourse (for example, that of a science) and other discourses (for example, those of other sciences) insofar as the same subject may consider several of them as making up his total discourse.

All these problems are concerned with the sentences of the discourse. But there may also be questions concerned with its terms—above all, if we exclude semantic considerations, the problems of the syntactical status of some among them.

18.   On the structural problems of RD

All the problems enumerated above arise in connection with RD. However, as was to be expected,
here they take a particular form because of the
peculiarities of this discourse. The structure of
RD is different from that of the discourse of science
insofar as authority does play a considerable role
in it; as a consequence, the logical nature of the
basic assumption is different from that met in the
sciences. This is one major difference between the
logic of religion and the logic of science.

Another difference is as follows: the discourse
of a science, especially when it is highly developed,
is constructed, so to speak, autonomously, that is,
without taking other discourses into consideration.
A physicist, for example, does not need, while con-
structing his system, to take into consideration the
everyday discourse he uses outside science. But the
situation in RD is different. For reasons which will
be discussed later on, RD is very closely connected
with the TD (total discourse) of its users, that is, it
cannot be disconnected and considered separately
from the PD (profane discourse) of the same subject. Therefore, the problem of the relations
between the two discourses, the RD and the PD, is
here particularly important.

We shall, therefore, have to examine the following questions:

1. What is the nature of the basic assumption
and heuristic rules in RD?

2. How is the objective content of RD structured, namely, what logic is used in the second axiomatic system?

3. What are the properties of the terms used? If we omit semantic considerations which belong to the next chapter, the main point to be examined here will be the syntactical status of "God" and related terms and expressions.

4. All these questions are concerned with RD itself; there is, however, a large class of problems about the relations between the content of RD and other classes of sentences. These problems will have to be dealt with next.

These problems may be discussed either in reference to a particular RD or in reference to RD in general. Although the study of a particular RD is proper to the logic of a concrete religion and would normally be carried on by the theologians of that religion—exactly as similar studies are carried on by scientists themselves—the study of RD in general belongs to general logic of religion and will have to be considered here.

19. On the general structure of RD

When we consider RD of the great religions it appears that it is always constructed in the following way:

1. First we find a class of object-linguistic sentences which are about the OR. This we shall call "objective faith," symbolically "p," and we shall call

its elements "ρ-sentences." ρ-sentences are what the believers directly believe; most of what is found in creeds, catechisms, and so on belongs to this class. "There is a God," "Christ is the Son of God," "Mohammed is the Prophet of Allah," "There is Reincarnation," are instances of such ρ-sentences. Objective faith corresponds to what we called in Section 17 "epistemic axioms"; they are sentences which are assumed by the believer without a further object-linguistic proof.

2. Second, there is a heuristic rule indicating which sentences are to be considered as elements of objective faith. It is a meta-linguistic rule and corresponds to the rule by which the axioms are enumerated in logical systems. It must indicate some characteristics of ρ-sentences, and, curiously enough, these characteristics are usually found to be syntactical. This certainly is the case in the Catholic religion, where it is possible to formulate the heuristic rule in purely syntactical terms, namely, by describing the form and the context in which elements of objective faith are to be found. In other religions, this rule is perhaps less precise, but there is always at least a tendency toward a syntactical formulation; this appears especially in the fact that in practically all religions there is a rule which says that whatever is contained in the Scriptures or in the creed of that religion belongs to the objective faith. Of course, the Scriptures usually need a lot of interpretation before they may serve as a basis

for the use of the heuristic rule; but, this being supposed, the rule can, in principle, be formulated in syntactical terms.

3. Third, there is the basic assumption, called here "basic dogma" ("BD"), a meta-logical rule, according to which every element of objective faith — that is, every sentence designated by the heuristic rule — has to be accepted as true. Thus a Mohammedan would admit that whatever has been revealed by Mohammed has to be considered as true; and a Catholic catechism says that whatever God revealed and the Church proposes to be believed is true, and so on.

At the same time, the BD also states something which is rarely explicit in it, but is known to be understood by all believers, namely, that all sentences designated by the heuristic rule have to be considered as possessing the probability 1. In most theologies it is even asserted that the certainty of the p-sentences is by far greater, indeed belongs to a quite different order, than the certainty of any other sentence. This, however, is a psychological matter; logically there is no probability higher than 1.

From the logical point of view, the situation in RD is very similar to that which we find in the discourse of natural sciences. The p-sentences play in RD a role closely similar to that of experimental sentences in those sciences. The only question which may arise in both cases is whether the given sentence really does belong to the class under consideration, that is, whether it really is a ρ-sentence, or a duly established protocol sentence. An enquiry concerning this circumstance is always possible and legitimate. But a quite general rule—namely, the basic assumption—provides every sentence which the subject is fully satisfied does belong to the said class with the probability 1.

Of course, the reason the basic assumption is made is different in the two cases. But this is a question which does not belong to the analysis of the structure of the discourse and which will be discussed at length in Chapter V. From the structural point of view the similarity is, with regard to this point, very striking indeed.

20. On the axiomatization of ρ

We will now proceed to our second problem, namely, that of the nature of the axioms in RD. As far as the epistemic axioms are concerned, the question is exhausted by what has been said in Section 19. However, the heuristic rule which permits selection of all sentences belonging to ρ does not permit the ordering of it. What the believer has as ρ is an unordered class of sentences. He is not bound by his faith to any axiomatization of that class.

But man is constituted in such a way that he always tends to axiomatize his discourse; and the religious man is no exception in this respect. There will be, consequently, a more or less pronounced tendency in believers to order the class ρ by axiomatizing it. Such an axiomatization is the field of what is called "theology" (or "Buddhology") in the strict meaning of the term; theology may, indeed, also have other tasks — for example, it may try to make the heuristic rule more precise, and to apply it to the given sources (Scriptures, and so on). But these are meta-logical tasks of theology and, by their very nature, marginal with regard to the object-linguistic task of axiomatizing the class ρ.

How will this axiomatization be accomplished? The theologian might proceed either by ordering the ρ-sentences alone, or by adding new sentences to them. Although theoretically the first method is not impossible, it seems often difficult to apply and, anyway, in historical practice the theologians frequently used the second method. This is also recommended by the circumstance that a considerable enrichment of the field may thus be achieved, as in all sciences.

But if this second method is applied, a question arises as to the logical status of the new sentences obtained in the system — logical as opposed to epistemological status, because from the epistemological point of view they will always be derived sentences (theological conclusions). Again there are two possibilities *a priori*: the theological conclusions may be obtained either deductively, or reductively, or in both ways. What the method of existing theologies really is has been little studied; yet the following provisional theorem may be perhaps 20.1   considered as well established empirically: *very few, if any, theological conclusions have been obtained deductively by the use of ρ-sentences only and purely logical laws and rules.*

Moreover, most theological conclusions seem to be established reductively. In other words, theology is more like physics than like mathematics. This may be seen in the following comparative table.

Physics	*Theology*
Starts (theoretically) with experimental sentences (epistemic axioms)	Starts (theoretically) with ρ-sentences
Explains the experimental sentences by other sentences from which the former may be deduced	Explains the ρ-sentences by theological conclusions which are such that from them the ρ-sentences can be deduced
Deduces from the explanatory sentences new ones which may be verified by experiment	Deduces from the theological conclusions new sentences, which may be verified by seeing if they do belong to ρ
Explains the first-grade explanatory sentences by further explanatory sentences in the same way	The same

Verifies such sentences by examining their consistency with other sentences in the system	The same
Introduces new "theoretical" terms not found in protocol sentences	Introduces new "theological" terms not to be found in p-sentences

The above view needs to be substantiated by studies in the logical structure of concrete theological work: such studies are unknown to the present author. The view suggested here assumes that the main task of the theologian is the axiomatization of objective faith and not the deducing of consequences from it.

21. On the logical syntax of "God"

We have next to consider the problems of the primitive terms of RD. Such terms offer many interesting semantic problems, but these do not belong in the context of this discussion; what is left are the syntactical problems of such terms.

From a grammatical point of view, RD is not unlike PD: it is composed of terms which may be grammatically divided into nouns, adjectives, verbs, and so on. A logical analysis at least of the theistic religions shows that, exactly as in PD, we may classify all terms of RD into arguments and different kinds of functors. These functors do not seem to offer any syntactical particularity. On the contrary, at least one basic argument is of syntactical interest, namely, the term "God" and analogous expressions in other languages and religions. This term plays a considerable role in RD; it has been said, and probably rightly so, that whatever is said in RD is about God in one way or another, that is, that all p-sentences assert a property of or a relation of God. Consequently, the syntactical status of "God" is of major interest for our study.

There are two possible hypotheses concerning this term: it may be either a name or a description. The first is possible only if the user of that term has a knowledge of God by acquaintance; if he does not have such knowledge, "God" must be an abbreviation for a description, namely, God is to such a man the subject which has such and such properties. In order to decide whether "God" is a name or a description, we must, therefore, consider the epistemological situation of the users of RD.

The class of those who use the term "God" may be roughly subdivided into two mutually exclusive subclasses: that of prophets who are the authors of the Scriptures and so on, and that of believers who are users of RD but not its authors.

As to the prophets, it is sometimes assumed by the users of RD that they had — at least in most cases — some direct experience of God. This means that they have a knowledge of Him by acquaintance —

and that, therefore, for them the term "God" is a name. It must be said that not all users of RD assume that all the prophets of their respective religions had such a knowledge; but at least for a subclass of them this may be admitted.

But as far as the believers are concerned, there are two opposed theories: according to one, every believer "meets" God every day, in every act of worship, and so on. The second contends that there is no such meeting of God by believers at all, and that at least the bulk of them have to "live on faith," "in the darkness of faith," without having any direct experience of God. According to the first theory, the term "God" will be a name for the believers. According to the second, it must be a description, that is, God is known by the believer only by some predicates applied to Him in the Scriptures. The partisans of the second theory would sometimes make some exceptions, for example, for the mystics; but this does not apply to the mass of believers.

The problem at hand has been still further complicated by the introduction of the term "religious experience" and the phenomenological studies of such experiences. It has been shown rather convincingly that, for example, in the act of prayer there is a so-called intentional object, namely, God, as the object of prayer; and the phenomenologists of religion, following Rudolf

Otto, often contend that there is a particular type of experience of such an object.

However, in spite of the nearly complete lack of serious empirical studies in this field, it seems that the great majority of believers, as they are now, do not have any real experience of God at all.

They pray and worship Him, but as they know Him, and nothing in their declarations suggests that in an act of prayer or other religious act they know anything more about God than what they learned from their creed. The only new factor seems to be purely subjective. But the creeds always describe God and cannot, by their very nature, convey a knowledge of Him by acquaintance.

21.1   On this assumption, we are entitled to state the following: the term "God," as used by the bulk of today's believers, is a description.

It is an abbreviation for a substitution in the formula

$$(\imath x)\ \{\varphi x\}$$

where "φ" is substituted by the product of the predicates attributed to God by the creeds concerned.

22. On the logical relations between π and ρ

We shall now consider the problems of the relations between PD and RD.

When we have two classes, the following products or sums result:

1. $\pi \cap \rho \quad = -(-\pi \cup -\rho)$.
2. $\pi \cap -\rho \quad = -(-\pi \cup \rho)$.
3. $\sim\pi \cap \rho \quad = -(\pi \cup -\rho)$.
4. $\sim\pi \cap -\rho = -(\pi \cup \rho)$.

5. $-\pi \cup -\rho = -(\pi \cap \rho)$.
6. $-\pi \cup \rho \quad = -(\pi \cap -\rho)$.
7. $\pi \cup -\rho \quad = -(-\pi \cap \rho)$.
8. $\pi \cup \rho \quad = -(-\pi \cup \sim\rho)$.

The following diagram represents the first four:

Among these eight classes, the following do not offer any difficulty, as the situations described by the theorems below are obvious.

22.2 2. $\exists! \pi \cap -\rho$.

The class of profane sentences which are not religious sentences is not empty. This implies in turn:

22.3 3. $\exists! \pi$.

The class π is not empty; there is—for each believer—a purely profane part of discourse.

22.4 4. $\exists! -\pi \cap \rho$.

The class of religious sentences which are not profane sentences is not empty. This implies again:

22.5 5. $\exists! \rho$.

There is, for every believer, a purely reigious part of discourse.

Consequently we have, by the general laws of logic, namely, by $\exists! \, (\alpha \cap \beta) \supset \exists! \, (\alpha \cup \beta)$:

22.6   6. $\exists! \, \pi \cup -\rho$.

22.7   7. $\exists! \, -\pi \cup \rho$.

Also by (3) we have:

22.8   8. $\exists! \, \pi \cup \rho$.

However, two other theorems offer some difficulties, namely:

1. $\exists! \, \pi \cap \rho$, that is, $\exists! \, -(-\pi \cup -\rho)$

4. $\exists! \, -\pi \cap -\rho$, that is, $\exists! \, -(\pi \cup \rho)$

Also, the class

$$\pi \cup \rho,$$

if it does not present special problems as to its non-empty character, is interesting because of the logic used to order this sum. Consequently, we shall have to deal in the following chapters with:

1. $\pi \cap \rho$.
2. $-\pi \cap -\rho$.
3. $\pi \cup \rho$.

23. On $\pi \cap \rho$

The first problem which occurs here is: is there a non-empty product of these classes, that is, is "$\exists! \, \rho \cap \pi$" true?

The situation of a believer may be described in this respect as follows. He admits as true a great number of sentences for reasons other than the basic assumption of his RD, namely, the elements of π. He also recognizes as true all elements of ρ. The elements of ρ are characterized by the absolute certainty which is carried by the act of faith, and the reason for this certainty is a very peculiar one; it is a religious reason, to be discussed later on. However, the same subject has many different reasons for assuming as true the different elements of π; and the degree of certainty of such sentences is variable, according to the method used for their justification.

The question arises, then, whether one and the same sentence may be recognized, at the same time, by a subject for religious and for profane reasons? If that be the case, the product of ρ and π would be non-empty.

It has been contended that this is impossible for psychological reasons. For, as has been said, an element of ρ is assumed on faith; consequently, it is not known, but believed to be true; whereas every element of π is supposed to be known and not believed, at least not believed for religious motives.

However, psychological considerations are often misleading in such matters, and it is better to consider the situation from a purely logical point of view. Here it appears as follows:

There is a sentence, say P, which is a theorem in π; can it also be a theorem in ρ? The logician must ask: and why not? It happens very often in human discourse that one and the same sentence is a theorem of two different systems with quite different sets of axioms, both of which are admitted by a subject. In the case of the believer we have to do with a logical sum of two systems, and the complete set of his axioms includes both the axioms of π and the fundamental principles of ρ. Now there is nothing logically impossible in the idea that the same theorem P may be deducible from one subset and also deducible from another subset of the same set of axioms, even if these subsets are mutually independent. We may, for example, very well imagine the situation in which a sentence about the age of the earth could be logically obtained both in the system of astronomy and in that of geology, both systems being recognized as correct by the same subject. This is the logical situation.

But even from the psychological point of view the arguments in favor of $\rho \cap \pi$ being empty are not convincing. They would be, perhaps, if the term "known" were understood—as Aquinas used it—in the strict Aristotelian sense, namely, as meaning a knowledge such as supplied by Platonic mathematics (rigorous deduction from evident axioms). But only elements of a very small subclass of π are known in such a way. Most of what we know is only probable. There seems to be no difficulty in admitting as true the following product: "*A* recognizes *P* as most probable for scientific reasons and A recognizes P as certainly true because of his faith" — which is the normal situation in such cases.

23.1   We state therefore that the logical product of ρ and π need not be empty.

24. On $-\pi \cap -\rho$

The other problematic class in the field of RD is the class complementary to the sum of π and ρ. The problem consists in knowing whether that class is empty, that is, whether there is an absence of sentences that are neither π- nor ρ-sentences. One would be tempted, first, to believe that such a class must be empty, because it could be argued that every asserted sentence of a given discourse is either a ρ-sentence, or a non-ρ-sentence and, if so, a π-sentence.

However, if the class ρ is defined as above (Section 19), the last premiss is unwarranted. We did define ρ as being that class of sentences which constitutes the objective faith, that is, those sentences which are designated by the heuristic rule. This means that ρ is the class of sentences which belong to the Creed of the given religion. But, if so, a sentence which is not a ρ-sentence does not need to be a π sentence; it may belong to still another class which is not identical either with ρ or with π.

This can be seen in the following way. The class ρ is a finite class and contains a rather limited number of well-described sentences. Only those sentences which are designated by the heuristic rule, and no others, are elements of ρ.

Let us now consider a sentence Q which (a) is not an element of ρ, and (b) has been derived from some elements of ρ (perhaps with some elements of π) by use of some logical rules. Such a sentence is obviously not an element of π. And this entails that there is outside π and ρ still a third class to be considered, namely, the class of sentences derived from elements of ρ. We shall call that class $\tau' \rho$. It has the following properties:

24.1
24.2

$$1. \quad \tau'\rho \subset -(\pi \cup \rho).$$
$$2. \quad \exists! \, \tau'\rho.$$

Property (2) is obvious from what we know about RD, that is, as far as is known, there is no RD in which there would not be some elements of $\tau'\rho$; for the believer is not content to sustain only the elements of ρ, but always makes some derivations from them.

But, if so, it follows that

24.3

$$\exists! \, -\tau \cap -\rho.$$

The class of sentences which are neither elements of π nor elements of ρ is not empty.

$\tau'\rho$ offers some interesting logical problems, which have been discussed historically under the title of the "problem of theological conclusions." The main question debated was whether an element of $\tau'\rho$ may be considered, as such, to be an element of ρ and, if so, under what conditions.

Now, strictly speaking, if only sentences falling under the heuristic rule belong to ρ, no element of $\tau'\rho$ can belong to ρ, except if it happens to be an element of ρ by that heuristic rule. For the rule does not say, in any of the known cases, that the sentences derived from ρ-sentences do belong to ρ, that is, that $\tau'\rho \subset \rho$.

However, it may be supposed—and seems at times to have been supposed—that such an additional rule is implicit in the heuristic rule.

Yet even if this be assumed, a distinction must be made between the different rules used to derive an element of $\tau'\rho$ from an element of ρ, and also between cases in which all premisses serving to derive a sentence are elements of ρ and cases in which at least one of them is not. There will be, therefore, three different cases:

a. The rule of derivation is infallible, and the premisses are

> a1. All in ρ.
> a2. Some in -ρ.

b. The rule of derivation is fallible.

To begin with case (b), it should be clear that a sentence derived in this way cannot be an element of ρ. The reason is as follows. The believers ascribe to all elements of ρ the probability 1, by the definition of faith. But no conclusion drawn by means of a fallible rule can have the probability 1; therefore, a sentence derived by a fallible rule cannot be an element of ρ. As much seems to be generally agreed.

But the two other cases seem to be controverted. In case (a2) we may still distinguish according to the probability of the elements of $-\rho$ used in the derivation. If that probability is less than *1*, the same argument applies as above and no sentence derived in this way can be an element of ρ. We are left, therefore, with only two possibilities: when the rule is infallible and when the premisses are either (1) all in ρ or (2) some are in not-ρ, but all have the probability *1*.

This problem, it must be insisted, is a problem of pure formal logic. There is no use trying to solve it by introducing any psychological or ontological considerations. For the question is one of consequence, and what can be yielded by consequence is a purely logical problem. But if it is, the problem of the formal logic of $\tau'\rho$ is stated and must be discussed in some detail.

25. On formal logic of $\tau'\rho$

Once formulae in which elements of both ρ and π appear are present, and this is above all the case in $\tau'\rho$, the problem of the sort of formal logic to be used arises.

Traditionally, as far as is known, this problem has never been raised by any author; they have all constantly supposed that the only sort of logic which is used in RD and also in theology or Buddhology, is classical bivalent logic. This is curious since at least some of the writers on the subject knew of other systems, namely, that of modal Aristotelian or Theophrastan logic.

However, if one considers the situation in $\tau'\rho$, the hypothesis that this must be ruled by another sort of logic is highly probable. For, contrary to profane discourse, TD quite obviously contains two classes of sentences, π and ρ, to the elements of which, apparently, different values are attributed. Thus, in Catholic writings sentences are not simply divided into true and false but, in addition to these, there are faith sentences *(de fide)* and heretical sentences. The logical situation may be described by the following theorems (where "*F(P)*" stands for "*P* is a faith sentence", "*T(P)*" for "*P* is a true sentence" and, "~*P*" for "the negation of *P*"):

25.1	(1) $(P) \cdot F(P) \supset T(P)$,
25.2	(2) $(\exists P) \cdot \sim F(P) \cdot T(P)$,

with the derived theorems

25.11	(1.1) $(P) \cdot F(\sim P) \supset T(P)$,
5.22	(2.1) $(\exists P) \cdot \sim F(\sim P) \cdot T(\sim P)$.

Now the most natural and simple interpretation of those formulae is supplied by the assumption that we are dealing here with a modal or multivalent logic.

This does not imply that one has, in order to

explain RD, to admit any philosophy of non-classical logic.One may as well be of the opinion that non-classical logic can be interpreted as more complex formulae of classical logic or, perhaps, use meta-logic instead. But the above statements show at least that it is not possible to deal adequately with logical problems of $\tau'\rho$ without using a more complex logic than that presented in classical textbooks.

Among others, the use of some modal or multivalent logic seems to be the only way to deal with the problem mentioned in the preceding paragraph, that is, with the question if $\tau'\rho \subset \rho$.

26. The structure of TD

We are now prepared to examine the logical structure of what we shall call the "total discourse"(TD) of a believer. This is the logical sum of his PD and RD, both classes being non-empty. First of all, the TD is stronger than the PD of a given believer.

This is obvious, for none of the elements of ρ which are a subclass of RD is derivable from the PD; also, inversely, there is no way of obtaining all the axioms of the PD from the ρ-sentences alone.

But when we consider the internal structure of the two classes, we see that, both from the methodological and from the epistemological point of view, they are far from being homogeneous. On the contrary, both comprehend different levels, characterized by a different logical status in the system and, consequently, by a different probability.

On both sides we may distinguish — as was said above (Section 17) — the basic assumption, the heuristic rule or rules, with application of the heuristic rule or rules, the basic sentences, the rules of derivation, and the derived sentences.

1. The basic assumption. This is, in RD, the basic dogma discussed above, and, in PD, a rule which says, for example, that whatever has been perceived directly is to be admitted. Once again, we must stress that the justification for these rules is different in RD and PD but that formally their status is the same.

2. The heuristic rules. In RD this is the rule which determines which sentences fall under the BD. In PD we have, on the contrary, a rather comprehensive set of methodological rules which determine the conditions under which a sentence has to be considered as an experimental sentence. It is a well-known fact that not every sentence which purports to be experimental is recognized as such in science; one condition, for example, is that it must be established by a trained observer, and so on.

3. The basic sentences. In RD these are the p-sentences; in PD the protocol sentences and similar directly verifiable sentences, obtained by application of (2).

4. The rules of derivation. Both in RD and in PD these are logical rules, some of them drawn from the logic of deduction, others belonging to reductive logic. They have different degrees of strength and yield results of different probability, according to their nature.

5. Derived sentences. In RD these are the elements of $\tau'\rho$; in PD they are all sentences which are not verifiable by ovservation but have been derived from (3) by use of (4).

Such is the general structure of the TD of a believer. He has, consequently, to deal with ten different sorts of sentences and rules. As we see, TD is a great deal more complex than PD or RD alone, as many new relations arise in TD which are not present in any of its subclasses.

We may now ask ourselves what the epistemological situation—or, speaking logically, the probability—is of the different elements of the TD? The answer seems to be the following:

1. The basic assumptions of both discourses are assumed axiomatically, and the corresponding sentences are held to have the probability *1*. Epistemologically, no doubt whatsoever is permitted about them.

2. The same is true, in principle, of the heuristic rules. However, as these rules, contrary to the basic assumptions, are usually complex, it may not always be clear whether the rule has been correctly

formulated and, especially, correctly applied. Consequently, there may be doubts about this factor, and a rational enquiry into its correctness may be effected.

3. If we suppose that the correct heuristic rules have been correctly used, then the results that is, the basic sentences, are again exempt from doubt. The principle *contra factum non valet argumentum* applies strictly, then, to the basic sentences of the PD, and a similar principle, *contra propositionem fidei non valet argumentum*, applies to RD. In common language, they are facts about which no doubt can be had once it is established that they possess the respective characteristics.

4. The rules of derivation are of two sorts, infallible and fallible. As far as the infallible rules are concerned, they yield certain conclusions only if they are really logical rules and have been correctly applied; consequently, even here a doubt is admissible. This is even more the case with fallible rules because their cogency is always imperfect.

5. Finally, the probability of the derived sentences will depend on all that has been said above under (2) through (4). These sentences are not exempt from doubt with regard to any part of our general scheme.

This general situation in TD is represented by the following schema, in which the points open to doubt and investigation are marked by an asterisk.

PD	RD
1.1. Basic profane assumptions	2.1. Basic dogma
1.2. Rules of selection of experimental sentences	2.2. Heuristic rule
*1.2.1. Application of 1.2	*2.2.1. Application of 2.2
1.3. Experimental sentences	2.3. ρ-sentences
*1.4. Rules of derivation	*2.4. Rules of derivation
*1.4.1. Application of 1.4	*2.4.1. Application of 2.4
1.5. Derived sentences	2.5. $\tau'\rho$-sentences

27.   On inconsistencies in RD

An amazing amount of astonishing things have been said both by believers and non-believers about the inconsistencies in RD, among which many sorts of "dialectics" and theories of "paradoxes" (that is, doctrines according to which RD is inconsistent) are the most conspicuous. However, most of what has been said is due to a nearly complete lack of understanding of the basic principles of logic.

It may very well happen, as a matter of fact, that there are contradictions in a given discourse; such cases are well known in every discourse and not just in RD. The discourse of science is, in particular, conspicuous in this respect.

However, the normal attitude taken by men when they meet with contradictions in their discourse is to try to overcome them. This may be done by two methods: (a) by a linguistic analysis of the terms used, (b) by an enquiry into the correctness of the assumptions (both logical and other). The reason why this attitude is assumed is that a contradiction, if admitted, results in meaninglessness of the discourse.

Moreover, the normal attitude toward the contradiction has been formulated by Whitehead in his famous statement "A contradiction is not a failure; it is an opportunity." The practice of science shows that the discovery of contradictions usually leads, because of the effort made to overcome them, to new and fruitful developments in the system.

But if such is the normal attitude in PD, there is no reason why another attitude should be assumed in regard to RD. RD is a discourse and, as such, it is subject to the general laws of formal logic.

This being assumed, let us see how inconsistencies may arise in RD and how they may be dealt with. We may distinguish, as to the first question, three different cases: the inconsistency may appear either in ρ alone, or in RD (that is, in the logical sum of ρ and $\tau'\rho$), or in TD (that is, in the logical sum of the RD and the PD of the subject).

1. If an inconsistency seems to be present in ρ alone, there are two ways of dealing with it: first, we may ask ourselves whether it is an inconsistency; second, we may ask if the two sentences under consideration are really ρ-sentences. Many apparent inconsistencies may be solved by the first

method. One instance is that quoted above: "The Father is God; the Son is God; yet the Father is not the Son." The inconsistency is present under the condition that the "is" appearing in the first two sentences is reflexive and transitive; but must it be interpreted as such? In this case there is, in the frame of this RD, even a deductive proof that the "is" is not transitive. It runs as follows: (1) If "is" as used here is reflexive and transitive, there is an inconsistency in ρ; this can be proved by means of classical logic; (2) there is no inconsistency in ρ; this is one of the assumptions of every meaningful RD. (3) Therefore, "is" as used here is not reflexive and transitive.

The second method consists in an enquiry as to whether the sentences in question are really in ρ; we may have been mistaken in supposing that they are, that is, we may have wrongly applied or wrongly interpreted the heuristic rules.

2. If an inconsistency is present in the logical sum of ρ and $\tau'\rho$, in addition to the two methods mentioned under (1), we may still enquire into the nature of the rule by which a sentence belonging to $\tau'\rho$ has been derived; if this rule is fallible and we are, on the other hand, satisfied that the other sentence is really a ρ-sentence and that its terms have been rightly understood, then of course the $\tau'\rho$-sentence must be rejected and there is no further problem. If the rule used is, however, infallible, then we may only ask if it has been rightly

applied. It may be mentioned that such inconsistencies are proper to theology.

3. If the inconsistency is one appearing between an element of RD and an element of PD, several different situations may be logically present: the element of RD may be either a ρ-sentence or a $\tau'\rho$-sentence; if it is a $\tau'\rho$-sentence, the rule by which it has been derived may be fallible or infallible. Further, the element of PD may be either a basic sentence (for example a protocol sentence) or a derived sentence and, if derived, it may be derived by fallible or infallible rules. When considering the schema in Section 26 we immediately see how many possibilities of enquiry are present in each case, that is, in how many ways the conclusion that there is an inconsistency may be erroneous. We are not going to examine them all, but we will enumerate the possible sources of error in the most complex case, namely, that case in which one of the contradictory sentences is a $\tau'\rho$-sentence, and the other a derived sentence of PD, obtained by fallible rules. In this case we must see: (1) whether the ρ-sentence from which the $\tau'\rho$-sentence has been derived is really in ρ; (2) whether the rule by which the $\tau'\rho$-sentence has been derived is an infallible rule and, if so, whether it has been correctly applied; (3) whether the basic sentence(s) from which the π-sentence has been derived is really a basic sentence; and, if not, (4) what the nature of the rules of its deriva-

tion is. There may be one rather interesting case, namely, the case where the rules which serve to derive the $\tau'\rho$ and the PD-sentences under consideration are both fallible. Then the degree of probability obtained on both sides must be weighed before one of these sentences is discarded.

One famous case in this field is that of Galileo. This believer (Galileo was one) thought that the sentence under consideration (namely, that the sun is revolving around the earth) is not only not a ρ-sentence, but not even a correctly derived $\tau'\rho$-sentence (in which he was right); at the same time, he thought that the Copernican theory (one of the implications of which was the sentence "the sun does not revolve around the earth") was obtained from basic sentences by infallible rules (in which he was wrong). His adversaries thought, however, that the first sentence was a ρ-sentence (in which they were wrong); and concluded, therefore, that the Copernican sentence must be rejected. An interesting position was taken by Cardinal Bellarmine; he suggested to Galileo that everything would be in order, if he, Galileo, would admit that the rules by which Copernicus derived his theory were not infallible.

28. Para-religious discourse

In most religions we meet with a phenomenon which still complicates the logical structure of RD. It seems that a rather large subclass of the believers of such religions admit not only the elements of ρ, $\tau'\rho$, and π, but also another class of sentences which do not seem to be included in any of these classes. One classical instance is that of the followers of some local minor prophet or saint; it seems that such phenomena are the most frequent inside the various religious (Catholic, Orthodox, Islamic, and Buddhist) orders—but there are also broader groups, like those who accept the sayings, for example, of the late Theresa Neumann. That part of the discourse of persons belonging to such groups which is not contained in their ρ, $\tau'\rho$, or π classes we shall call "para-religious discourse."

What is the structure of para-religious discourse, and what are the logical relations between it and the other parts of the RD of the persons concerned?

We note, first, that they have a sort of peculiar basic assumption of their own; for example, in the example quoted above it will be formulated approximately as follows: "for all P, if P has been asserted by Theresa Neumann during her periods of prophecy, then P is true." This being assumed, para-religious discourse has a structure similar to $\tau'\rho$. This much seems to be clear.

But what are the logical relations between the para-religious discourse and the RD proper, as defined by the respective churches? One hypothesis is the following: the basic assumption of para-religious discourse is derived from a ρ-sentence or some ρ-sentences with the help of some π-sentences. In this case, this basic assumption will really be a part of $\tau'\rho$, at least in the intention of the believers concerned. However, there will be one major difference between $\tau'\rho$ and this assumption: namely, that, although the elements of $\tau'\rho$ are object-linguistic sentences, the elements of the latter (the para-religious assumption) are meta-linguistic rules, by means of which, in turn, object-linguistic sentences are derived. The situation in both cases can be illustrated by the following schemas:

RD

Basic dogma
↓
Heuristic rule

|
|
↓
ρ

RD and Para-Religious Discourse

Basic dogma
↓
Heuristic rule
／
Para-religious
(meta-linguistic)
assumption
↓
ρ Object-linguistic
para-religious
sentences

IV

Meaning in Religious Discourse

The theory of meaning in RD is that part of LR which has been, relatively speaking, the most studied in recent years, especially in Great Britain, under the influence of the analytic school in philosophy. As our purpose is, however, to offer a survey of the problems occurring in the field of LR as a whole, it has been thought useful to insert a chapter on meaning too, the more so because several questions seem not to have been examined or even noticed by other authors.

This chapter will be basically a study of semantics applied to RD. Some of the semantic problems of this discourse have already been treated in Chapter II (Sections 10–11) because the very legitimacy of a LR depends on the solution of some of them. But there are many other questions still to be examined. We shall deal with them in three parts:

In the first, we shall make a comparison between semantics and hermeneutics of Sacred Scripture, in order to make clear the purpose of the present study (Section 29); then the main classes of problems will be stated (Section 30).

In the second part, the problem of meaning of ρ-sentences, namely, their verifiability, will be examined. After some generic considerations on meaning and verification (Section 31), we shall study the theories according to which the ρ-sentences are verifiable indirectly, either by authority (Section 32) or by reduction (Section 33), and directly (Section 34).

The third part will be devoted to the meaning of ρ-terms. We shall first state the problems at hand (Section 35) and analyze the notion of mystery (Section 36). Then two different theories will be examined: the theory called "Negative Theology" (Section 37), and that of Analogy (Section 38).

29. Semantics of RD and hermeneutics of the Scriptures

There exists a vast body of writings by theologians and Buddhologists of various religions concerned with the explanation of the meaning of the Scriptures. A properly enormous amount of work has been done in that field by Christian theologians of various confessions, and many are the opposing schools among them. It may be, therefore, legitimately asked: by what right is a logician going to study meaning in RD without being himself a specialist in that hermeneutics? For the Scriptures are obviously an important and basic part of every RD; and without a thorough analysis of the discussions about them, it seems a highly risky enterprise to engage in the study of religious semantics.

This seems, however, to be a misunderstanding. As a matter of fact, the object of a semantic study, as conducted by a logician, is quite different from the object of a semantic study conducted by these theologians. He works on a different level, one which presupposes that the work of hermeneutics is already done. This can be seen in the following way.

What the students of hermeneutics are concerned with may be legitimately compared with the logically fundamental part of the work of the historian, that is, dealing with documents, not with observed facts (as the observer in physics does). Moreover, even a physicist who works with protocol sentences established by other men is in a far easier situation than the historian, as he can take the meaning of these protocol sentences for granted, which the historian cannot. The historian has to decipher, so to speak, the text he has at hand, to understand first what the sentences really mean, and then how far they can be considered as reports about facts. Similarly, the student of a given Scripture must decipher it before he gets at the p-sentences he is after. Take, for example, a parable: the hermeneut must establish, first, that it is a parable; then he must try to find out what it really is supposed to mean; only then can he say that he has found a sentence or a set of sentences belonging to the ρ of his religion. This is a very simple example; we know of many far more complex ones — but the scope is always the same: the theologian tries to find the "real" ρ-sentences behind the text he has at hand.

But the logician, as has already been said, supposes this work already done. He does not have to deal with the sacred Scriptures and their perplexities. He supposes that he meets clear-cut ρ-sentences. Although acknowledging the merits of the men who prepare his work, he is not directly interested in it. He works with the ready-made ρ-sentences alone.

It may be asked, however, whether this procedure is legitimate. Are there such sentences? Can the work of hermeneuts be considered as already performed? Fortunately, the following may be said: at least some authentic ρ-sentences are present in an unambiguous way in every religion. It is true that some theologians seem to speak as if for them there were no such sentences, as if everything in their religion was quite problematic. But the logic of religion is not interested in the private beliefs of such theologians; it studies religions as great social phenomena and, in them, the

29.1   RD of the masses of the believers. Now these believers most certainly do believe some determined sentences and suppose that they have been quite clearly obtained from their respective Scriptures. The creeds of all religions contain a large number of such sentences, and logic of religion has to deal with them.

These very sentences offer, however, a number of semantic difficulties of a quite different sort than those met by hermeneutics. In connection with them the general problems of meaning and verification do arise, as they do in reference to every propositional discourse. And as every propositional discourse has its own particularities, so also has the RD. The study of these particular semantic problems of ρ-sentences and of their parts is the subject of this chapter.

It is not suggested by what has been said here that such problems are never studied by the theologians of various religions. Indeed, they often are. However, when theologians conduct such studies they are performing the work of a semanticist.

30. The problems of meaning in RD

It has been shown above that believers intend to use RD meaningfully; more precisely, that they intend to communicate objective structures through some parts of RD (Section 12) and among others, propositions (Section 13). So much is taken for granted here.

But the statement of this intention of the users of RD is not the solution of problems of its meaning. On the contrary, these problems arise only when this assumption is made — as it must be — about the intention of the users of RD. This chapter is devoted to the analysis of some of these problems.

Why are there special problems of this sort in RD? Because RD is supposed by its users to be about a transcendent object — the OR — whereas RD is itself composed of terms which are all either terms of profane discourse or are defined by using such terms. These two facts must be analyzed first of all in order that the problems at hand might appear clearly.

1. The object of religion, that which RD is about, is said by all its users to be transcendent. By this the following is meant:

a. The OR is not a possible object of sensuous experience. It cannot be perceived by the senses.

b. It is not even given to the believer in the fashion in which the object of phenomenology is said to be given. It is not a phenomenon in Husserlian terminology.

c. It has not a single property which would be specifically the same as any property known in natural experience.

d. The propositions about the OR are said to be held "by faith" and are not established in the way in which scientific propositions, or such propositions as are expressed by everyday language, are established.

This is what is usually meant when users of RD

say that the OR is "quite different" from any other object. In some theories of RD, the "otherness" of the OR is made still greater. But the properties enumerated above are sufficient to show the difficulties with which the semantics of RD will have to deal.

2. The RD in which believers do talk about the OR is exclusively composed of terms which are also terms of PD or are defined by such terms. This is obvious to everyone who considers the Scriptures and the Creeds: we find in them not a single term which is not either a term of profane language or defined by such terms. In other words, formally speaking, RD is in no way different from scientific discourse, which, as is well known, is entirely composed either of terms belonging to everyday language or of terms defined by such terms.

This being so, two major problems arise as to the meaning in RD: first, the problem of the meaning of its terms; second, the problem of meaning of its sentences, that is, of the method of their verification.

a. The problem of meaning of religious terms. It should be clear, from what has been said, that the terms used in RD do not have the same root meaning as in PD; for if they did the OR would have properties possessed by other, natural entities, which is denied by what has been said about this object.

b. The problem of meaning of religious sentences. Even if we suppose that the meaning of the terms composing a ρ-sentence is known, the problem of the method of verification of such ρ-sentences is not yet solved. Given the nature of the OR and of faith, none of the criteria usually applied in order to decide about the truth of sentences in PD can possibly be applied. It follows that the users of RD apply some other criteria of meaning. The problem is to know what those criteria may be.

The order will, however, be inverted here; we shall first analyze the problem of verification of religious sentences, and then only the far more complex and difficult problem of meaning of the terms in such sentences.

31. On meaning and verification

A sentence has meaning if and only if there is a method of verifying it; by "verifying" is meant an activity by means of which one is able to decide whether a sentence is true or false. This principle is evident in itself: to understand what a sentence means is possible only on the condition that one knows when it is true or false. However, it has often been misstated. Two such misstatements may be mentioned here, in order to avoid possible objections.

a. One consists in saying that the meaning of a sentence is the method of its verification. This statement is inconsistent with a normal use of the terms "meaning" and "verification." For no sentence can be verified apart from its meaning—in other words, only a sentence which already has meaning can be verified, and not a mere string of words without meaning. It follows that meaning cannot be identical with the method of verification. Our principle, however, does not assert that they are identical: it only states that "P has meaning" and "there is a method of verification of P" are equivalent, which, in the frame of intensional logic (and we have to deal with such a logic), does not entail that they are identical.

b. Another misstatement consists in restricting the method of verification to sensuous perception; a sentence is said to have meaning if and only if there is a method of verifying it by sensuous perception. This statement is indeed not inconsistent, but it is quite unwarranted and, in any case, it restricts the class of meaningful sentences so much that many sentences become meaningless even in empirical science. Our principle, again, does not assert such a restriction: in order that a sentence be meaningful there must be some method of verification, and not necessarily a method of verification by sensuous experience.

We may ask: what is the logical status of the principle itself? The answer is that it is analytical; that is, it is entailed by a set of sentences describing what is usually meant by "meaningful." Given such an analytical definition of "meaningful" (by the said set), the principle follows analytically and is not an affair of convention.

However, the principle contains several terms which need explanation, because they are ambiguous. There are two such ambiguities in particular.

1. "There is a method of verfying P" means the same as "P can be verified" or "There is a possibility of verifying P." What possibility? H. Reichenbach distinguished among the technical, physical, and logical possibilities. There is a technical possibility when we are in possession of technical means of verifying. Physical possibility exists whenever a process of verification is, in principle, not inconsistent with the laws of nature, in spite of the fact that we may not have, as yet, technical means to utilize it. Finally, logical possibility is present whenever the sentence "P has been verified" is not inconsistent with the laws of formal logic.

2. When we say "P can be verified" one may legitimately ask: by whom? The following possibilities occur:

a. By every human being. In this case very few sentences would be meaningful, indeed. I cannot verify now, for example — at least technically — whether Kilimanjaro really exists, and most people are quite unable, even if they had the necessary apparatus, to verify what our physicists tell us about the structure of the atom.

b. By at least one man. Suppose that a person A

is the only person in the world who has sufficient mental capacity to verify the correctness of a certain train of reasoning K. On that assumption the sentence "the reasoning K is correct" would still be meaningful.

c. By any intelligent agent, whatever it may be. In that case even sentences which cannot be verified by any human being would be meaningful, if there were the possibility of verification, say, by a Bodhisattva, or an Angel, or by God.

3. In addition to these two ambiguities, which are implicit in the principle, there is still a third one, stated explicitly: namely, the ambiguity expressed by the formula "a method of verifying." We may ask: Is any conceivable method permissible, or should we restrict the class of such methods, and, if so, in what way? For there are different methods of verification. Even in physics the direct inspection of phenomena must be distinguished from indirect verification by reasoning. But if we pass from physics to other sciences, for example, to psychology, there may be other methods still— for example, introspection. We may roughly divide all possible methods of verification in the following way. First, there will be direct and indirect methods, the indirect being ultimately based on some sort of directly verified sentences. Direct verification may be again divided into sensuous and non-sensuous. Finally, non-sensuous verification may be divided into natural (possible to man

in his natural state) and supernatural (assumed as possible for another state).

$$\text{Verification} \begin{cases} \text{direct} \\ \text{indirect} \end{cases} \begin{cases} \text{non-sensuous} \\ \text{sensuous} \end{cases} \begin{cases} \text{natural} \\ \text{supernatural} \end{cases}$$

This being said, the question occurs: on what grounds is a concrete criterion of verification and, consequently, of meaning chosen? The exclusion of some criteria may be justified by deduction in a given frame of reference. For example, if one operates within a frame of reference in which no non-sensuous perception is admitted he will be entitled to reject all direct criteria other than those of sensuous experience. Similarly, if one rejects the existence of a state other than the natural state for man, he will have to reject the supernatural criteria.

Such cases are, it seems, the most relevant; at any rate they are most relevant to our subject. We may further ask, therefore, on what grounds is the frame of reference referred to assumed? In some cases we quite clearly have to do with purely pragmatic reasons. For example, when a physicist assumes a frame of reference in which no non-sensuous perceptions are admitted, he does so because this assumption has proved to be of great utility in physics. There may be, however, cases in which the choice is made not because of pragmatic motives, but as a result of some theoretical reasons. For example, it seems certain that many among those who reject every supernatural religion do so because they reject the possibility of a non-natural perception; and this, in turn, they contend, they do on some theoretical grounds.

The business of the logicians is, however, not to decide whether such reasonings are right or wrong, and less still whether basic religions or quasi-religious beliefs (such as the last cited) are correct. His only interest in this part of logic is to determine what criteria may be used in a given discourse on logical grounds.

32. On indirect verifiability of ρ-sentences by authority

There often exist quite precise criteria by which a believer knows or may know whether a ρ-sentence is true or not in the frame of his RD. The nature of these criteria have been discussed in the preceding chapter of this study. Here it will be enough to state that all these criteria depend on the concept of legitimate authority. This concept is analyzed in an appendix to the present book.

This being so, the first hypothesis concerning the method of verification of ρ-sentences is that this is indirect and consists in showing that the given sentence fits the given criteria, or is the negation of a sentence which is true by those criteria.

This offers an interesting semantic problem. Suppose a sentence P, which cannot be verified by one person, say *A*, can be verified by another person, say *B*, and suppose further that *A* lacks not only technical means of verification but even understanding of the methods by which *B* verifies *A*. Such cases seem to be frequent today, for example with regard to certain laws of physics and the non-physicists. Is, then, *P* still meaningful for *A*? It seems it is not. There is, however, a difficulty. Many persons in the situation of *A* would still think that *P* is true, provided that *B* enjoys sufficient authority with regard to them and to the field to which *P* belongs. Now one could say that, if *A* asserts *P* as true, then *P* must be meaningful for *A*. The answer consists in an analysis of "true" as used in the above sentence. All that is meant here is that *P* must be asserted by everyone who has the knowledge of *B*, and nothing else. As far as *A* is concerned, *P* remains completely empty for him. This is, in fact, the way in which we often do accept some scientific sentences without knowing what they mean. More, we do so even in cases in which we not only do not understand the method of verification but even the terms of which *P* is composed.

Can this be the situation arising with ρ-sentences? Of course it can and, doubtless, often has occurred in the history of religions. It has happened, and still does frequently, that the believer accepts a sentence without having any understanding of it, simply because he believes that it has been asserted by the Revealing Agency. But is it possible to say that such is the situation with all p-sentences? The answer is that it is not. For if this were the case the whole content of objective faith would be empty for the believer. Now this is certainly not consistent with the real attitude of the believers: at least some among the p-sentences seem to be believed in all religions as properly meaningful. One instance is the sentence "There is a God" in theistic religions. It is hard to imagine that this sentence is taken to be an empty formula, to which the believer does not attach any meaning at all.

32.1   The conclusion seems to be that there is no way of verifying the p-sentences by authority.

33.   On indirect verification of p-sentences by reduction

There is, however, another possible hypothesis about the method by which p-sentences are supposed to be verifiable. It will be explained later on that a believer may admit, before the act of faith, a sentence which we shall call the "religious hypothesis." It will be argued that the content of the act of faith is not different (materially) from that of the religious hypothesis. Therefore, one may think that this content—namely, the sentences of which the creed is composed—is verifiable in the same manner in which a scientific hypothesis is, indirectly by reduction. The fact that the religious hypothesis does contain some terms which do not occur in the experimental sentences forming its logical basis does not matter much—for many scientific hypotheses do contain so-called theoretical terms which are of the same nature. Consequently, one may think that, if it may be said that scientific hypotheses—especially such as are arrived at by second-degree induction—may be accepted as meaningful, exactly the same, and by the same sort of criteria, may be said about the content of faith, that is, about the ρ-sentence.

But this solution will not do.

There are, as has already been said, two ways of conceiving of the principle of verification. One we shall call the "conventionalistic way." We then establish by a purely arbitrary convention what sort of sentences, and under what conditions, we shall consider as meaningful. Any method chosen will then do the job; we may, for example, decide that the possibility of transforming the given sentence in a given way is sufficient as its verification. The other way, which we shall term "analytic," consists of limiting the class of possible methods of verification to those by which a real (psychological) understanding of the meaning may be obtained.

Now it is true that many contemporary methodologists seem to use the conventionalistic approach. But it also seems that in our field this will not do. The question as to whether a given sentence is meaningful or not cannot be answered by the believer by invoking a purely arbitrary rule. What is required is something which will supply his sentences with a meaning he can grasp.

If one accepts, then, the analytic point of view, it will appear that there is a fundamental difference between the way in which explanatory sentences of empirical sciences are verified and the way that has been suggested here for ρ-sentences. The difference is simply this: the deduction used in the first case is an object-linguistic deduction; it consists of a certain transformation of the sentences under consideration. For example, let Q be the explanatory sentence, the rules used be R and the basic (protocol) sentence on which Q is based be P. Then Q is obtained by transforming P (and some other sentences) by R, where R is based on logical laws. The consequence is that Q is a logical transformation of P and nothing else. But in the case of ρ-sentences the situation is very different. Here the deduction is meta-logical and the content, the structure of the sentences involved, is not directly pertinent. The basic rule states that: (P), if $P \in \alpha$, then P is true, where α is a certain class of sentences. In other words, the rule says that, whenever a sentence is affirmatively contained in a certain authoritative text, then this sentence is true. It is hard to see how, under such conditions, the verification by this rule could supply the sentence under consideration with meaning.

33.1   Therefore, it seems that no verification by the

BD, considered as a well-established hypothesis, is possible.

And this means that there seems to be no way of verifying the ρ-sentences indirectly.

34.   On direct verification of ρ-sentences

34.1   It follows, therefore, that the believers must assume some sort of direct verification of the basic ρ-sentences. As was said above (Section 31) this does not need to be taken as technically possible for the subject; it is enough that he might conceive of an intelligent agent which would verify the sentences under consideration. But this verification must be by some sort of experience. As it is usually assumed by the believers that this experience is not only non-sensual but even non-natural, this presupposes that the believers admit the possibility of a non-natural experience of some intelligent agent.

This presupposes, again, that the believer does not limit the possible ways of direct perception to **34.2**   sensuous or even to natural experiences. A thoroughly Humean view of knowledge seems, therefore, to be incompatible with the assumptions of the believer.

The following objection arises here. To verify a sentence P means to obtain from P (and other asserted sentences) some predictions which can in turn be seen to be true or false. For example, the sentence "My friend John sits in the other room" allows the deduction of the prediction "If I go there, I shall see him." Now these predictions must be, themselves, understandable for the subject. It must be clear from the beginning what is meant, for example, in our case by "seeing the friend." But in the case of supernatural verification the predictions are supernatural themselves; they consist, for example, of the sentence "If I die, I shall see God," and the very meaning of such words is not clear. Moreover, it looks as if a circle has been committed: we are verifying ρ-sentences by other ρ-sentences which equally need to obtain their meaning by verification.

It seems, however, that this objection is not fatal to the theory. It would be, if the seeing involved were an act of perception radically different from all acts we know. But this does not need to be the case. The supernatural verification must be supernatural in as much as the object is supplied in a supernatural way; but the act by which it is perceived does not need to be basically different from an act of intellectual vision, as practiced naturally, for example, in phenomenological intuition and other similar acts. If an—admittedly inadequate—comparison may be made, it is as if the sentence "There are yellow plants on Venus" could not be technically verified because we lack even the understanding of means by which we could get there; yet this sentence would still be meaningful because the act of seeing is something familiar, and the corresponding prediction "If I go to Venus, I shall see yellow coloring on plants" is fully meaningful.

35.   On Mystery

A term which frequently occurs when believers are speaking about the OR is "mystery." The OR is, they say, mysterious by definition, and even mysterious in a very peculiar, "higher," way. In order to obtain some degree of clarity as to the meaning of RD, it is, therefore, necessary to analyze the meaning of this term, which seems to be crucial to our problem.

The first step in such an analysis is to note that the adjective "mysterious" properly applies not to objects but to sentences. It is, of course, often said that, for example, God or Nirvana is mysterious, but RD abounds also in properly meta-linguistic statements, in which sentences are called directly not only "mysterious" but even "mysteries"; so there is talk about the "mysteries of the faith," etc.

Now "mysterious" in general seems to mean a state of affairs which cannot be completely grasped. More precisely, the sentence P is mysterious for a subject x if, and only if, x does not fully grasp P. But now the meaning of "grasp" must be clarified.

We find the following possible meanings:

1. P is mysterious for x if and only if x understands very well (even fully) the meaning of P, but he is unable to discover by his own means (insight

or reasoning) the truth-value of *P*. This means that *P* is accepted by *x* on authority only. He does not know that *P* is true; he just believes it on the authority of somebody. We shall call that sort of mystery "truth-value mystery."

2. *P* is mysterious for *x* if and only if *x* understands the meaning of *P*, so to say, in itself, but does not know its axiomatic connection with other accepted sentences. Then *x* does not have a full grasp of *P*, because this is always conditioned by the axiomatic context. This kind of mystery will be called here "axiomatic mystery."

3. *P* is mysterious for *x* if and only if *P* contains at least one term *a* such that *a* is used in *P* in a way only partly corresponding to the use of *a* in PD. This we shall call the "weakened-meaning mystery." In this case, something is still meant for *x* by *a* (and consequently by *P*), but the meaning concerned is somewhat weakened.

4. *P* is mysterious for *x* if and only if there is in *P* at least one term *a*, which is completely meaningless for *x*. This we shall call the "nonsense mystery."

The above are translations into the language of contemporary semantics of utterances which are frequently made by the theoreticians of RD among the theologians. It is often said, for example, (1) that the truth of the religious mysteries cannot be known, but must be believed. What is meant here is just this: their truth-value can be known only by religious authority, and not by any other means of justification. It is also said (2) that the words in which the truths of the faith are expressed do not exhaust the infinite wealth of their object, by which is meant that there is an axiomatic connection of the sentences under consideration with many other sentences, unknown to the subject. Third, (3) there are several theories which contend that the terms of RD are of such a nature that they convey only a part of the meaning usually ascribed to them in PD. Two instances of such theories are those of Negative Theology and of Analogy. And, finally, (4) the theory of the Unspeakable is often (and rightly) connected with the assertion that all terms of RD are properly meaningless.

One characteristic of all these theories (excepting the last one, which has been dealt with in Section 11) is that the limitations of meaning implied by the use of "mystery" or "mysterious" are said to be absolute, whereby it is understood that these limitations are due to the very nature of the OR and cannot be overcome by any man—contrary to what happens in PD, where there are many "natural," that is, limited and relative, "mysteries."

Of the four classes of theories concerning the Mystery, only the third needs to be examined here. The first is, as a matter of fact, just a statement about the structure of RD. The second offers no peculiarities, as similar situations also arise in

PD. Finally, the fourth theory has already been discussed above (Section 11). We are, therefore, left with the third class. Those are the theories according to which there is only a partial identity between the meaning of a term in PD and that of a term of the same shape in RD. As has already been said, the two main theories of this kind are those of Negative Theology and of Analogy.

36. Negative Theology

This theory differs from that of the Unspeakable. It does not contend that RD does not mean anything; it only asserts that whatever it means—and, according to the theory of Negative Theology it does mean something—is purely negative. It seems that no partisan of this view has ever made an attempt to formulate it in sufficiently precise terms; in its present vague form it is, of course, subject to many objections. Here are some of them:

a. There is an expression meaning that x is non-white. If this expression, as applied to the OR, is supposed to mean the negation of non-white, then it means that the OR is white, and we obtain a perfectly positive property.

b. If it is meant that we may say everything about the OR meaning its negation, then contradictions are entailed. For then we must ascribe to the OR the property of being non-white (the negation of the property of being white) and the

property of being not-non-white (the negation of
the property of being non-white), that is the property of being white; at least if one admits the principle of double negation.

c. If one attempts to limit the scope of the theory
to the class of positive properties, these properties
must be defined. But it is difficult to define a
positive property, and no satisfactory account of
them is known.

The first thing we must do here is to try to give
the theory some sort of precision. In order to do
so, we must attempt to define a positive property.
This may, perhaps, be done in the following way:

1. A directly perceived property is a positive
property.

2. A property defined by a formula containing
only symbols of positive properties and terms of a
positive logic is a positive property.

This is, of course, not very satisfactory. For one
thing, it restricts the class of positive properties far
beyond what is meant by the partisans of Negative
Theology. Then, it may be argued, the notion of a
directly perceived property is vague; why could
one, for example, not directly perceive that a cow
is not blue? As we have, however, far more serious
grounds for rejecting Negative Theology, let us
assume that in some way the class of positive
properties has been indeed correctly defined.

Now as to the precise meaning of the theory, the
following hypothesis does, perhaps, fit the inten-
tions of its partisans. Let *t* be a term used in any

PD. Then we may truly assert that what is meant by t does not apply to the OR. Writing "$M(t, \pi, \varphi)$" for "t is a term used in PD as meaning φ" and "α" for the class of positive properties, we obtain

$$(1) \qquad (F): M(t, \pi, \varphi) \cdot \varphi \, \epsilon \, \alpha \cdot \supset \, \sim\!\varphi(OR).$$

But what, then, does RD say? Well, it says that the OR does not have this and that, and other, properties, and this for all positive properties which are expressed by the terms of PD.

So formulated, Negative Theology does not entail any immediate inconsistency. For (1) ascribes to the OR a purely negative property, or at least not a positive property according to our definition above—as a negation has been used in the formula.

Similar to the situation which arises in the frame of the theory of the Unspeakable, the OR has been described here, namely, by the formula

$$(2) \qquad (\imath x)\{(t): M(t, \pi, \varphi) \cdot \varphi \, \epsilon \, \alpha \cdot \supset \, \cdot \sim\!\varphi(x)\}.$$

This is, contrary to what happens in the theory of the Unspeakable, not a meta-linguistic property (despite the fact that meta-linguistic terms are used in the description), but an object-linguistic property of second level. Again, similar to what happens in the theory of the Unspeakable every object-linguistic property of the first level is said not to be ascribed to the OR by RD.

But then the same objections may be made

against Negative Theology as those mentioned above (Section 11). If not inconsistent in the frame of general logic, it is inconsistent with the RD as a whole. For it is obvious that RD ascribes to the OR first-level properties, and several of them, in its propositional part; and, as far as its non-propositional element is concerned, it supposes that such properties are ascribed to the OR by those who use RD. The proof is the same as in Section 11. One cannot worship an entity of which he assumes only that no positive properties can be ascribed to it.

36.1   Therefore, the theory of Negative Theology as formulated here must be discarded.

37. On Analogy

Another theory of partial meaning is that of Analogy. The difference between it and the theory of Negative Theology is this: while in the theory of Negative Theology only negative aspects of what is meant by a term in PD are applied in RD, at the same time in the theory of Analogy some part of the positive meaning is preserved. Consequently, this theory can be formulated in the following way: whenever a term of PD is used in RD, the meaning it has in RD is partly identical with that which it has in PD and partly different. For example, when the term "Father," which is a term of PD, is used in RD, it means there something only partly identical with its meaning in PD. The important point by which this theory is distinguished from Negative Theology is, as was said, that the part of the meaning which is common to both uses is not exclusively negative, but also positive.

It will be easily seen that this sort of use of a term in two different fields is that which is commonly called its "analogical" use. When we say, for example, that a stone is heavy and that an obligation is heavy, the term "heavy" is said to be used in the latter sentence analogically to its use in the former. That is why the present theory has been rightly called the "theory of Analogy." There are, in medieval and Renaissance Catholic Theology a considerable number of studies on Analogy in RD, and some discussion about it has also taken place during the twentieth century. The ancient writings are an instance of purely semantic work done by theologians of one religion which applies equally to the whole field of LR. It is not our intention to enter into the details of that discussion, but to sketch the main problems which arise in this context.

The first and main problem is this: what is identical in the two uses of a term, that is, the term in PD and the term of the same shape in RD? On the level of general LR this question must be stated in categorical terms. It then can be formulated as follows: is that which is meant in the two discourses *absolute properties or relations?*

Both answers are *a priori* possible. However, in

most religions the transcendence of the OR is so much stressed that, quite naturally, most authors who have studied the problem have concluded that no (absolute) properties may be meant in common for the OR and for any object dealt with in PD—in other words, that which is common in profane and religious use of a term can mean only relations.

But, and this is the second problem arising here, even relations seem to offer a great difficulty in RD, because of the same transcendence. This can be seen in a concrete instance. Let us consider the term "Father." This term means in PD a set of relations studied by different sciences, in particular by physiology, psychology, and sociology. But it seems difficult to admit that any of these relations holds of God or of any other transcendent OR. God is believed to have no body and, consequently, no physiological relations. He is also thought to have no mind of the same type as human beings have; he is endowed with a "superior" mind, or even an "absolute" mind. Finally, it looks quite inconsistent to say that God has any social relations of the type studied by sociology. The conclusion seems to be that none of the relations which make out the meaning of "Father" in PD can be meant when one says that "God is the Father."

The result of this train of thought seems to be that we are pushed back to the theory of Negative Theology: for, if not even relations meant in PD can be meant by the same terms in RD, then what remains seems to be a set of purely negative properties.

37.1 However, there is also another possible hypothesis. This asserts that what is common in the two meanings are just the formal properties of relations. By "formal properties of relations" are meant properties which can be defined by purely logical functors. Instances of such properties are: reflexivity, symmetry, and transitivity.

If we apply this theory to the instance of "Father" we shall have to say that this term, when used in RD, means only the formal properties which are found in the realizations meant by "Father" in PD. In our case we have, among others, non-flexivity, asymmetry, and intransitivity.

The interesting aspects of this theory are the following:

1. It does not compel one to conceive of RD as meaningless.

2. It allows, at the same time, the assertion of an extreme transcendence of the OR.

3. And yet, it permits even very strict reasoning about it.

This theory will be formulated in some detail in a technical appendix.

V

Justification of Religious Discourse

In this last chapter the problems of justification in religion will be examined. After some general considerations of the possible methods of justification (Sections 38–39), the relevant problems will be stated (Section 40), and the various possible solutions enumerated (Section 41). The remainder of the chapter will be devoted to the examination of the respective theories (Sections 42–49).

38 On justification

We call "justification" the activity by which the acceptance of a (meaningful) sentence is justified. In general methodology a distinction is usually made between direct and indirect justification. The first consists of an act of (sensuous or non-sensuous) insight; the object must be always present. The second consists of a reasoning; the object is not present. There are no other methods of justifying the acceptance of a sentence. In particular, those who claim that a third method is the so-called pragmatic one are mistaken: because, when we use that method, we reason and thus the pragmatic justification is just a particular case of the indirect method.

Indirect justification is usually divided, with Aristotle, into deductive and inductive, the former being defined as a reasoning from the universal to the particular or singular, and the latter as the inverse process, from the singular or particular to the universal. It is, however, clear that this division is not exhaustive. There are, first, reasonings in which we proceed from universal to another equally universal statement; and there are reasonings in which we proceed from a singular statement to another singular statement. Instances of the former are many mathematical reasonings; and practically every reasoning of the historians offers an example of the latter.

It is, therefore, better to divide reasoning into deductive and reductive, according to the doctrine of Łukasiewicz, who himself claims to have taken it from Jevons. The distinction is explained by him as follows.

Every reasoning has as one premiss a conditional, or a sentence which can be easily transformed into a conditional. As the second premiss we use, in deduction, a sentence of the same shape as the antecedent of that conditional and obtain as conclusion a sentence of the shape of its consequent. In reduction we have as a second premiss a sentence of the shape of the consequent, and we obtain as conclusion a sentence of the shape of the antecedent of the first premiss. This can be represented by the following schemas:

Deduction	*Reduction*
$p \supset q$	$p \supset q$
p	q
———	———
q	p

Induction is clearly just one case of reduction, namely, the case in which for "p" a generalization of what is substituted for "q" is substituted. It should be clear also that reduction uses a non-infallible rule.

Although formal sciences are mostly deductive, empirical sciences use reduction as the basic method. This is (exactly as deduction) of two sorts: in the reasoning we may start either with the consequent or with the antecedent. In the first case we have explanation; in the second, the process is called "verification." The typical process of natural sciences consists first of explanation, by which an explanatory sentence is established (mostly a general sentence) — then of verification: new consequences are drawn from the explanatory sentence and verified.

The use of these methods of reasoning is by no means limited to the natural sciences. To mention just one case, court decisions are often based on reasonings of the same type; and among moral sciences, history is a typically reductive science in most of its parts. Deduction and reduction – explanatory or by verification – are, indeed, the most fundamental and general methods available in any field for justification if it cannot be obtained by direct experience.

39. On Authority

There is, however, still another classification of the methods by which a sentence may be justified. The indirect justification may use as premisses exclusively object-linguistic sentences or, among them, it may use at least one meta-linguistic sentence. We shall call the former method "object-linguistic" and the latter "meta-linguistic."

In meta-linguistic justification the procedure usually takes the following course. First, it is established (by deduction, reduction, or insight) that, whenever a sentence P has a certain contextual property φ, then P is true. Then it is assumed (again by proof or insight) that P possesses the property φ. It is then – deductively – concluded that P is true.

One instance of such meta-linguistic justification has already been mentioned, implicitly, in Section 17, when the structure of RD was discussed. For the elements of the objective faith are assumed to be true by the believer by the application of the heuristic rule. But this rule states that whatever sentence has a certain contextual property (for example, if it is to be found in the Scriptures) belongs to the said class. We have here, consequently, to do with a meta-linguistic justification. The ρ-sentences are justified meta-linguistically.

However, there are many other instances of such procedures, also in PD. One outstanding class of meta-linguistic justifications is that which uses authority. In this case, the following meta-linguistic sentence is assumed: whenever a certain person A asserts a sentence P, then P is true. It should be quite obvious that most sentences of which the PD of a modern man is composed are justified by authority. For the modern man must rely— and this more and more heavily with the progress of specialization—on the authority of the experts in various theoretical and practical disciplines. Because of this, there is, indeed, an urgent need to have a logical analysis of authority; curiously enough (perhaps under the influence of such superstitious slogans as "a rational man does not accept any sentence which he cannot justify himself, without recourse to any authority") this does not seem to have been done up to now.

We may now ask ourselves: What is the structure of a justification by authority? At least two premisses must be assumed in order that it may work at all. The first states that a certain person is an authority in a given field; the second, that a certain sentence has been asserted by this person and that it belongs to the field in question.

The question now arises: how can these premisses be justified? Obviously, each of them can be
justified by any of the three basic ways in which
man can justify a sentence at all—by insight, by
deduction, or by reduction. In the last two cases,
authority may again be used as one of the premisses. For example, if one admits that whatever his
doctor, whom he trusts, says about his disease, is to
be accepted as true, this premiss seems to be based
on a complex reductive reasoning yielding the
conclusion that, for every x, if x is a good doctor,
whatever x says about the disease of a patient he
has examined carefully is to be accepted as true.
This reasoning will be, so it seems, mostly inductive; and among its premisses there will again be
some sentences accepted on authority. In the case
of a child the authority of the mother may play a
considerable role in this situation.

It is, however, the direct justification of the first
premiss which is of greatest interest to us. This is
produced by a rather particular type of insight—
because it is an insight into some properties of a
person. This sort of insight is usually called
"trust." If we analyze what "trust" may mean in
this context, we find that it is an insight into the
truth of two sentences:

1. A knows the situation in the field in which A
is an authority.

2. A speaks truthfully about the elements of that
field to the subject.

To say that *S* trusts *A* in our context means precisely that *S* believes (1) and (2), There may be, indeed there must be, some emotional, phenomena accompanying the acceptance of (1) and (2), but from a logical point of view the only relevant point is that (1) and (2) are accepted by *S*.

It is important to grasp the fact that the acceptance of (1) and (2) does not need to be based on any reasoning. The "trust" described may completely replace it. When a child trusts his mother or a lover his beloved, there is probably some sort of insight into the person of the partner which yields the certainty on the basis of (1) and (2) — and no reasoning is needed.

40. The problem of justification of RD

The nature of the problem of justification in religion has often, it seems, been misunderstood, that is, insofar as many writers have primarily been concerned with the justification in RD itself, namely, inside the system, and not with the justification of the RD, namely, of its basic assumptions. Of course, there is one striking difference between the justification of ρ-sentences in RD and that of many analogous sentences in PD. This consists of the fact that the procedure is always meta-linguistic in RD, whereas it is often object-linguistic in PD. But this is, surely, a minor difference and the less relevant since in some parts of PD meta-linguistic justification is also used — for example, in historiography.

It must, therefore, be stated that the way in which the single ρ-sentences are justified inside a RD, that is, when the BD (like the heuristic rule) are already accepted, is not problematic at all from the logical point of view. Here we have to deal with quite classical justification of a set of sentences with the use of another set of sentences, by deductive or reductive means, and these are methods where RD hardly differs from PD.

On the contrary, the way in which the basic assumption of RD, that is, its BD, is accepted by believers, does offer some interesting logical problems. They arise because of the sharp distinction believers usually make between knowledge and religious faith, science, and religion. They are taken to differ not only as to their objects and, consequently, as to their vocabularies, but also, it seems, as to the way in which the basic assumptions of each field are accepted. This being so, we may legitimately ask the following questions:

1. Is the BD of an RD justified at all?

2. If so, how? Or, in other terms, given that there is a difference between justification in RD and in PD, what is that difference?

These are the problems to be discussed here. It must be remembered that we are dealing with problems of applied logic, and therefore that we are trying to carry out logical analysis of a material which is empirically given. However, as has already been mentioned in the introduction (Section 4) our situation is rather precarious in so far as we have very few empirical studies about the linguistic behavior of believers. This handicap will be particularly severe in this chapter. In order to be able to analyze the phenomena as they really are and not our own theories, we need a far more elaborated empirical basis than that which we have.

It looks as though the majority of the writers on the subject have analyzed either their own personal behavior in RD or, what is still worse, their own views of RD. This danger is present to a high degree in this enquiry also.

For this reason, it will be necessary to proceed with great care and to try to limit the enquiry to those aspects which are either completely *a priori* or, although empirical, seem to be quite obviously present in the behavior of the mass of believers. Because of this restriction, the results will have to be modest. It is, however, better to offer modest results with a relatively high degree of probability than ample results with little probability.

41. Theories of justification

As to our first problem, there are two classes of possible theories which answer it: either there is no justification of the BD or there is some. The first class contains just one element, which will be termed here (1) "the blind-leap theory." The second class contains, on the contrary, a number of different theories, resulting from the different answers to our second problem, and depending on the various sorts of justification available to man, enumerated above (Section 38). They may be expressed in the following schema:

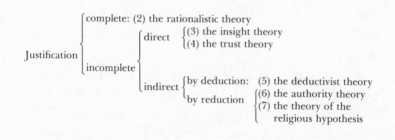

Here is a short statement of these theories:

1. The blind-leap theory. There is no justification at all of the BD. The believer makes a "leap" from nothingness, to full faith without any logical or experimental foundation.

2. The rationalistic theory. There is a complete justification of the BD—be it by natural insight, deduction, or reduction; nothing else is necessary for the acceptance of the BD in the way a believer does accept it. In opposition to this theory, all those listed under "incomplete justification" admit only a partial justification; the result of such a justification is not yet the BD as it is accepted by believers, but there is need for another act (that of faith).

3. The insight theory. The believer has an insight

into the truth of the BD; this insight—so it seems—must be supernatural.

4. The trust theory. According to this theory, the BD is based on trust in the Revealing Agency (in theistic religions, of God) itself.

5. The deductivist theory. Insofar as the BD is justified, it is justified by purely deductive reasoning, with premisses which are ultimately based on insight.

6. The authority theory. Here the rational activity preceding the act of faith uses human (and, consequently, natural) authority as a premiss. This leads, later on, to the assumption of the authority of the Revealing Agency; however, there is no insight into this as is assumed in the trust theory.

7. The theory of the religious hypothesis. The believer constructs, on the basis of experimentally known premisses, an explanatory hypothesis. This hypothesis becomes the BD after the act of faith has intervened.

41.1   Of these various theories, it seems that the third, namely, the insight theory, has never been seriously defended and does not merit consideration. It should be clear that the BD of every religion is by no means a necessary sentence and, at the same time, it has an utmost generality. Such sentences cannot be justified by direct insight, not even in part. We shall, therefore, omit an examination of this theory. The rest will be studied in the order indicated above.

42. On the blind leap

According to this theory, the believer does not have any reason to believe, that is, to accept, the BD as true. The act by which he accepts it is often characterized in this theory—somewhat poetically—as a "leap." The would-be believer does not know anything about the truth-value of the BD in question at a time t_1; then he makes the "leap" mentioned and, without any insight or proof, he accepts the BD; at a time t_2 he becomes, by that leap, a believer. It is vain to look for any justification of his act.

This theory is usually justified as follows: we do make a distinction between knowledge and religious belief, between science and faith. But science is characterized by the fact that no sentence in which it is expressed is accepted without some reason. Consequently, faith must be characterized by the circumstance that the sentences in which it is expressed are accepted without any reason, by an act of will, utterly unjustified and unjustifiable.

Some partisans of this theory have gone so far as to deny the justification of the elements of objective faith by the BD, or even to deny that there is any propositional content in RD at all. We dealt with these misunderstandings elsewhere (Sections 13 and 14). They are, however, irrelevant for the present purpose. The problem under consideration is whether the basic dogma, assumed to be a (metalinguistic) sentence, is justified in any way or not.

This problem is an empirical one. As has already been stated, we would need, in order to study it accurately, a far more systematic basis in empirical research than we factually possess. However, the general situation seems to be well enough known that we might tentatively state the following theorems:

42.1   1. *It seems highly improbable that the majority of human grown-up individuals are able to accept any sentence as true without having at least some justification for that acceptance.*

This seems to be the more the case when sentences are concerned which are considered important by the individual in question. Indeed, the agreement about this seems to be so general that individuals who admit as true sentences that they consider important without justification would be thought mentally abnormal.

2. *Believers do as a rule behave so that it may be legitimately assumed that they have at least some reason for accepting their BD.*

That is, they are usually prepared to argue in one or another way in favor of their religious beliefs, which means that they can produce some justifications of their BD. These justifications are, indeed, very different according to the religion and to the individual, but it seems clear enough that some justification is always present.

42.2   But if this is so, the blind-leap theory, as formulated above, must be discarded; it is contradicted by overwhelming experimental evidence.

If we give to this theory the following form:

(1) For all *x* and *y*: *x* does not supply the BD with the degree of justification *y*,

its rejection entails:

(2) There is at least one *x* and one *y* such that *x* supplies the BD with the degree of justification *y*.

That is the provisional result of the present discussion: according to what we know about the behavior of the believers as a mass (and not about the theories offered by some theologians), there is some justification of the BD in each religion.

43. On Rationalism

The rationalistic theory is not the contradictory of the above blind-leap theory but its contrary, and is consequently far stronger than the result obtained in Section 42 under (2). Although the negation of the blind-leap theory entails only the assumption that there is some justification of the BD, which might be a partial justification, the rationalistic theory contends that there is a full justification of it. This is not to be interpreted as meaning that the believers obtained by this justification a full certainty (comparable with that of direct insight or of convincing deductive proof). It is, however, essential to it that the acceptance of the BD by the believer is solely and entirely determined by the rational justification he has of it. The term "rational" refers in this context to natural insight, deduction, and reduction, with the last two assuming naturally known premisses.

It seems that there are two different kinds of such theory. The first, which we shall term the "strictly rationalistic theory," claims that all premisses used in such justification are factual, that is, of the same sort as those assumed in science. The second, which will be called here the-"broadly rationalistic theory," would also accept as premisses sentences expressing moral and esthetic propositions, which we shall discuss when examining the theory of the religious hypothesis (Section 48).

Of these two theories, the first seems to be flatly contradicted by experience. For if the situation were such as the first theory claims, then there would be no difference, in principle, between RD and PD, the sentences in PD being justified precisely in the way this theory claims to be the only one acceptable for RD. But it seems obvious that there is a difference between RD and PD; and this consists not only of the vocabulary used, but also, and perhaps above all, in the fact that the way in which its sentences are accepted is widely different from that of the sentences of the PD. In face of this, it is hard to see how this theory—the rationalistic theory—could be rationally sustained.

In contrast, the broadly rationalistic theory does not meet with so much difficulty. It admits, as possible premisses in the justification in RD, sentences which are not admitted in the justification of the sentences of PD, or at least of those of science. For science deals exclusively with factual sentences (even if it talks about values, it considers them as facts). So there would be a difference in the manner of justifying sentences of each field.

However, this theory also meets with great difficulties if we consider the situation as it really is in religious communities, and not merely *a priori*. We find, then, that the distinction between faith and knowledge, and by this it seems that the ways of justifying both are meant, goes farther than what is assumed by the broadly rationalistic theory. It seems to be not only a difference of the kind of premises assumed but, above all, a difference as to the result of the justification. Although in PD there is no other factor needed after the act of justification has been performed, in RD, after all has been done in the way of justification, we still do not have what believers call "faith." Something more seems to be required.

If we consider the linguistic behavior of the believers we usually find the following statements concerning "faith":

1. It is said that faith is distinct from science because there is no "proof"—which means, it seems, full justification—in faith and there is in science.

2. It is also said that "faith is free," by which must be meant that there are no compelling rea-

sons to accept it and that the decision as to its acceptance is an act of choice.

3. Faith is said to carry with it a certainty which is (a) of a different nature from that of science and (b) much higher than the latter.

Those facts can be best explained, it seems, in the following way:

43.1   1. There is some justification of the BD.

43.2   2. This justification is not quite conclusive, so as to leave the subject who utilized it free to accept or not to accept the BD so justified.

43.3   3. After the BD has been justified rationally in the above way, the believer-to-be performs another act by which this very BD obtains the certainty mentioned above under (3).

43.4   4. Only after this act, which is called the "act of faith," has been performed does the subject become a believer and his relevant discourse a RD.

It must be stressed that logic is not interested in the act of faith as such; it is, however, interested in whatever precedes it in the way of preparatory justification. For justification, as understood here, is always a matter of logic, that is, of methodology, which is one of the major parts of logic.

But other sciences may be rightly interested in the act of faith. We may mention here, first, psychology of religion; second, phenomenology of religion; and third, the various theologies or Buddhologies of the religions concerned. The theologies are interested in the process because, depending upon which religion they are studying, a supernatural factor in faith is usually admitted. Faith is said to be produced by human will with the help of divine grace, or by illumination by Buddha, and so on.

This had to be said for two purposes. On the one hand, it must be shown that it is not the business of logic as such to interfere with the work of these other sciences, in particular that of theologies and Buddhologies, except insofar as it may examine the correctness of their reasoning. For logic as such cannot assume any p-sentences and cannot, therefore, be competent in any such field. On the other hand, the statement may be useful to clarify a point which does not always seem to have been understood: namely, that every attempt to substitute psychological, phenomenological, or theological considerations for logical analysis is illegitimate here. When justification is concerned, it must be repeated, logic alone is competent, and no other discipline.

44. The trust theory

The trust theory of religion asserts that the acceptance of the basic dogma is directly justified by the trust in the Revealing Agency, for example, in God. No reasoning at all is involved in the justification, but a sort of emotional insight into the situation which is precisely called "trust." The partisans of this theory, too, have sometimes gone so far as to deny any propositional content to p-sentences, identifying the content of faith with this trust. This is, of course, a wrong assumption; but even if we admit, as we have (Section 13), that a believer does accept the truth of a proposition expressed in a sentence, the theory of justification by trust alone remains a possible solution of our problem.

In order to avoid possible misunderstandings, it must be remembered that we are not dealing here either with the justification of p-sentences inside the system, that is, on the basis of the BD, or even with the justification of the BD by indirect methods, for example by reduction. The trust theory, as understood here, is a doctrine according to which the BD itself is justified by a direct trust in the Revealing Agency.

The paradigmatic situation used by the proponents of this theory is that of a child who accepts with trust whatever its mother tells it. There is no reasoning here, just a sort of insight into the person of the mother, associated with strong emotions. Suppose the mother says to the child: "There is a town called 'New York'." The child trusts his mother so much that he strongly believes that there really is a town called 'New York.' Of course, we may say that there is an implicit reasoning of the following form:

(1) For all P, if A says P, then P is true.
(2) A says P.
(3) P is true.

Yet both premisses have been accepted here without reasoning — the first by trust, the second by direct experience. This is what this theory means, and this is also what it asserts of the situation in RD.

The most important point here is (1). We may ask what the necessary conditions are in order that (1) might be accepted. Well, according to the theory itself, there must be the trust in the mother. But you can trust only a person whom you know to exist. So the sentence

$$(1.1.) \;\; A \text{ exists}$$

is one necessary condition of (1). Moreover, the premiss (2) must also be known to be true, independently of the authority of A. Both (1.1.) and (2) may be known by direct experience or some sort of reasoning; but, in any case, they must be known before the conclusion can be obtained.

Now in the case of our child, the situation is clear: that child knows by direct experience both (1.1.) and (2). But in the case of religion, the situation is different.

We may distinguish here two different situations:

A. The Revealing Agency has manifested itself only to the prophets and through the Scriptures.

B. The Revealing Agency reveals itself also directly to each believer in such a way that its existence may be perceived and that the content of its message may be directly understood by each believer.

44.1   In case A, the trust theory is unacceptable. The two conditions needed are missing—there is no direct presence, and there is no direct knowledge of the message. The trust may, indeed, operate later on, but only when the believer has already justified by other means—mostly by reductive reasoning, usually assuming some human authority—the fact that the Revealing Agency exists and that it has revealed what is believed by him.

It is sometimes said that the believer believes with trust, *at the same time* and in the same act, the existence of the Agency, the fact that it did reveal a certain proposition and this very proposition. However, this clearly entails a vicious circle: the existence of the Revealing Agency and the fact of Revelation is justified by an operation which presupposes both.

In the case B, on the contrary, there is no logical difficulty in the theory. The decision as to its acceptance is a matter of factual experience. We may ask ourselves, namely, whether there is such constant and universal direct communication of propositions by the Revealing Agency to each believer. This question could only be answered if we had enough empirical studies concerning the mass of believers. We do not possess such studies and cannot, therefore, have any scientific certainty as to this point.

This author's personal opinion is that the theory is wrong on empirical grounds. It seems to him that there is no such continuous Revelation to the mass of believers but that they are "living in the darkness of faith," meaning that whatever Revelation there is, is communicated to them by the Scriptures and Creeds. The believer, it is thought, starts with written sentences which convey some message, communicated (according to his faith) to some Prophets many centuries ago; he does not personally meet God, except perhaps when he is one of those saintly men or women sometimes called "mystics" in RD. This is, however, just a personal opinion which would have to be substantiated by empirical studies. It may be, however, noticed that the opposite doctrine has exactly the same status: it is just a personal opinion and nothing more.

45. The deductivist theory

Historically, the deductivist theory seems to have been prevalent among the theologians during considerable periods of the history of religions. As far as the Western (that is, from the point of view of logic, Greek) world is concerned, this was largely due to the deductivist attitude nearly universally accepted under the influence of Aristotle's *Posterior Analytics*. Science, and this meant true knowledge, is, according to that work, arrived at either by insight or by deductive proof. Outside science there is just opinion, *doxa*, which is quite inferior to true knowledge. Now religions claim a supreme kind of knowledge, a *gnosis,* for their tenets. The temptation to conceive of it as deductively obtained lay very near, as there was no way to achieve a direct insight into the truth of p-sentences.

In this attitude we may still distinguish two different trends. One of them, which might be termed "radical," conceives of RD as being established by deductive means with such a degree of certainty that RD is more firm than any other discourse, or at least equally as firm as, because of the proofs supplied. The other, more moderate, does not go as far as that. It admits that there is in RD an element which is not demonstrable; but whatever is demonstrable in RD is demonstrable by deductive proof.

The theory runs approximately as follows. The believer first proves the existence of God by purely deductive means. He then proves, by means which are supposed to be equally deductive, that God did reveal some propositions, namely, those contained in the Creed. Third, the believer demonstrates, again by deduction, that God (a) knows everything, (b) cannot reveal false propositions. It then follows that the content of the Creed is true. It has been demonstrated by deduction starting with evident premisses.

From a purely logical point of view there is only one major objection to this train of thought:

namely, that no historical sentence can be demon-
45.1 strated by deduction; consequently, it is simply
impossible to have a purely deductive justification
of religion in the above fashion.

Therefore, this theory is not of much interest
for the present enquiry. However, it merits some
consideration because its rejection entails one
rather important conclusion: if there is justification of BD neither by insight nor by deductive
proof, the result of such a justification cannot have
that sort of certainty which is obtained by the
method of deduction. The reasoning used here
must be reductive—and every reductive reasoning
consists of an application of fallible logical rules; it
cannot yield, consequently, certainty. As a result,
what has been said above about the incompleteness
of every justification of BD is confirmed. For the
45.2 BD is accepted by the believers as absolutely certain, whereas every sort of available justification
produces only a sort of probability of less than 1.
In fact, this has often been called in traditional
writings about our problem a "moral certainty" and
considered as lower than that obtained by insight
or deductive proof and, especially, as lower than
the certainty of faith.

46. The authority theory
This theory asserts that the BD is justified by authority. The authority used here is, however, not
that of the Revealing Agency, but a human au-

thority. That such an authority does play a role in justification of the BD in many cases is quite certain. Whether it does supply all justification in all cases is another question.

There are two logically quite different ways in which such a method may be used, according to the justification of the authority itself. These are, namely, direct or indirect.

1. In the direct case, no reasoning is used in justification: the human authority which serves as a premiss in the justification of the BD is itself directly justified.

2. In the indirect case, human authority, accepted as a premiss, is itself justified by reasoning, and sometimes even by a rather complex reasoning.

Case (1) probably always occurs with children and, it seems, in compact human groups where the authority of the group is accepted without any doubt. Case (2) is that of a believer who himself has undertaken some historical studies on the origin of the Scriptures and of the Creed of the religion concerned and has concluded that the authors of such texts are to be accepted as authority in regard to the BD.

1. The first case does not offer major difficulties. The believers behave in that respect exactly as they do in other fields; it is a well-known fact that children and members of the above-mentioned compact groups rely heavily on the authority of their parents or of the groups to which they belong.

Insofar as RD is concerned, nothing seems to occur here which would differ from the behavior in PD. This merits stressing because sometimes the justification of the BD of religion has been presented as specifically different from many other justifications by the same subjects.

There is, however, one phenomenon which seems to have different characteristics in our field. It happens that some individuals accept the authority of a person who is neither their parent nor an authoritative member of the social group to which they belong. This is the case in religious conversions made under the influence of a preacher or prophet of a religion. This phenomenon is the more important in that most great religions were at a certain time new religions and must have started their careers as social bodies when a number of individuals were converted, that is, when they accepted the authority of some prophet or preacher. Moreover, similar phenomena are familiar even today.

The logical analysis of this phenomenon offers some difficulty because the psychological analysis seems to be insufficiently performed. The following remarks may, however, be made.

It may happen, first—and, indeed, it seems to happen normally—that the prophet or preacher presents to his hearers the religion he preaches in a way which corresponds to their needs—by which we mean that he offers it as an explanation of their experiences, exactly as we shall describe it while analyzing the religious hypothesis (Section 48). If that is the case—and insofar as it is the case—we really do not have to deal with authority, but with a justification of the BD by object-linguistic reduction, which has to be discussed later on.

Second, it may happen—and again it seems that it does normally happen—that the hearers are attracted not only by the content of the preaching, but by the person of the preacher. In other words, they get a sort of insight into his person which directly establishes for them the truth of the sentence: "Whatever this preacher says about religion is true."

And if this is true, there is basically no logical difference between this phenomenon and the well-known phenomena of accepting the authority of parents or of the social group. In both cases there is, of course, much to be said by psychology; but, from a logical point of view, no further problems arise.

2. In the second case, the believer does not accept any authority of persons or social groups he knows by acquaintance, among others, of any prophet or preacher of religion. The authority he relies on is that of writers who usually have lived many centuries ago, especially the authors of the Scriptures. It is important to notice that in that process he does not act as a believer, that is, he considers the Scriptures as purely profane documents and his reasoning is not based on any ρ-proposition. This does not prevent him, after he

becomes a believer, from ascribing to the same Scripture a religious character. But in the first stage the reasoning is exactly of the same kind as all historical reasonings in PD.

That reasoning must yield as a conclusion the premisses of the same type as those needed to establish any authority, namely, that the person in question did exist, that he did write the texts concerned, and that he is to be trusted in that field. How can this be established? The existence of the author must be justified by historical, reductive, reasoning; the same applies to the authenticity of the texts, where methods of reasoning used in literary criticism must be applied; finally, similar procedures are to be applied in order to establish whether the author has authority in his field.

It is not denied that in some cases reasonings of this type may yield highly probable conclusions. However, it seems that in the case of the Scriptures, all arguments—even the best—which may be brought to bear are relatively weak. In no other way of justifying the BD does there appear as clearly as here that there is a considerable difference between the certainty of the faith and even the highest probability which can be obtained by justification.

47. On crisis of authority

Both in religion and in other fields there often occurs the question of the crisis of authority. By this a process is meant whereby a subject who up to a certain time has relied completely on authority feels doubts about it and tries to obtain a more rational justification of his views. By "more rational" a method must be meant in which authority plays either no role at all or a lesser role than before.

47.1   It will appear from what has been said that the terms as defined are ambiguous, that is, that the crisis of authority may take at least two different forms.

1. First, a passage from the first case to the second described in Section 46 may be meant. Up to a certain time the subject relied on the authority of his parents, of his social group, or of a prophet or preacher whom he knew by acquaintance. He now desires to make a personal enquiry into the truth of the BD and therefore studies the Scriptures of his religion in order to determine their authenticity, authority, and so on. If as a result of such studies he still remains a believer, he has not dropped authority as a means of justification. He has only replaced the authority known by direct insight by an authority established by reductive reasoning.

2. But, second, a more radical "rationalization" may take place—and, it seems, very often does take place. The subject wishes then to discard every human authority. In doing so, if he remains a believer he passes from the justification by authority to a justification by an object-linguistic method. Of course there are cases in which he

ceases to be a believer, but these are outside the scope of the present enquiry. We are interested only in those cases where, after the religious crisis, that is, after the rejection of every authority, the subject remains a believer. This entails his now having a quite different sort of justification of his BD.

There may be, indeed, cases in which the crisis leads to a reacceptance of authority. This happens when the subject has obtained by certain reasonings a new justification of that authority. However, the cases in which all human authority is rejected, and yet the subject remains a believer, seem to be present and merit discussion.

It is suggested that in such cases a reductive, object-linguistic justification is used. It is indeed highly probable that such a justification does play a role and even a considerable role with many believers quite independently of the crisis of authority. It is, that is, very probable that, for example the members of compact social groups which rely primarily on the authority of these groups for the justification of their BD also secondarily use the reductive, object-linguistic method. For the religion in question is, to them, not only what has been taught by their elders; it is also a certain view of the world and of existence which explains their experience — and this is a justification of one's BD by object-linguistic reduction.

Such a reduction consists of establishing a religious hypothesis. The theory concerning it is the most interesting in this field; it is also one which offers the most difficult and, as yet, unsolved logical problems. We are going to deal with it now.

48.   On the religious hypothesis

This theory has been voiced many times by different theologians mostly under misleading titles such as "pragmatic justification," and so on. It needs to be restated in logical terms in order to avoid the severe misunderstandings which may occur in the context. So reformulated, the theory is this: the believer constructs before the act of faith, as an explanatory sentence, the very BD of the religion concerned. This sentence—called here "religious hypothesis"—serves to explain his experience. Psychologically, it is not identical with the faith; but it has the same content as the act of faith bearing on the BD.

Formally, the procedure by which the religious hypothesis is established is closely similar to that used in reductive sciences. The starting point is experimentally established sentences. The hypothesis is of such a nature that they may be deduced from it; it permits predictions and can be verified by new experimental sentences deduced from it.

However, there are two major differences between the religious hypothesis and any explanatory sentence of the sciences:

1. The basis, that is, the class of the experimental sentences which form the starting point, is far

more comprehensive; whereas in every science we have to deal with only one subclass of experimental sentences recognized by the subject, the religious hypothesis seems, in some way, based on all sentences accepted by him, on his total experience.

2. This basis seems to include not only factual sentences, that is, sentences referring to facts, but also esthetic and moral sentences, that is, to sentences on moral and esthetic values. This is probably the reason why the correspondent theological views have been called "pragmatic"; for sentences about moral values have a direct relevance to action.

The procedure is conceived as follows: at a certain time of his life the subject begins to think that, if he does accept the BD of a certain religion, then the whole of his experience will become organized and somewhat explained. This is what writers probably intend to say when they assert that it "gives a meaning to the world and to existence." Logically this means that the religious hypothesis plays the role of an axiom out of which the remainder is thought to be deduced (with the help of other sentences, of course). After this hypothesis has been formulated, it is verified by considering other different experimental sentences accepted by the subject.

This nature of the religious hypothesis explains two curious phenomena occurring in RD: on one hand, the difficulty of persuading another man of its truth, and on the other, its very solidity, that is, the difficulty of overthrowing it by falsification. The first phenomenon is explained by the fact that no two persons have the same total experience; and, consequently, a hypothesis which seems to be quite plausible to one of them does not need to appear plausible to the other, that is, related to his experience. The difficulty in overthrowing a religious hypothesis by falsification is again explained by its extreme generality. It is a trivial truth that the more general an explanatory sentence is, the more falsification it can take without being overthrown. One must be very little instructed in the procedures of science to think that a dozen facts inconsistent with a great physical theory will lead automatically to its rejection. But the religious hypothesis seems to be by far more general—that is, it covers far more sentences—than even the most general scientific theory. Therefore, it is much more difficult to overthrow it. It can be done, of course, but there must be quite an amount of falsifying evidence.

49. Problems of the religious hypothesis

That believers do, at least in many cases, formulate a religious hypothesis, seems quite certain. This means, as has been said, that they do explain something by it and that the hypothesis helps them in making some predictions; for these are the two major characteristics of every hypothesis.

This much can, consequently, be taken for granted It is, however, not easy to say, what this hypothesis explains and how it allows predictions. The difficulty in solving those two problems is perhaps partly due to our lack of convenient logical tools; above all, it seems to be caused by our insufficient knowledge of the factual reasoning in believers.

As far as the first problem, that of explanation, is concerned, at least four different cases may be conceived of. The religious hypothesis may, namely, (1) explain factual sentences only, (2) co-ordinate the factual sentences with value sentences, (3) explain value sentences only, (4) explain sentences about specific religious experiences.

1. The first case, as a matter of fact, never occurs. As far as is known, every religion, and consequently every religious hypothesis, serves—at least collaterally—to explain some value sentences also. That is one reason why every religious hypothesis is different from a scientific hypothesis. However, many cases in the history of religion are known in which this plays above all the logical role of an explanatory sentence for factual sentences. In this case, it is very similar to a scientific hypothesis of great generality. It may be that during periods in which there was no science at all, or very little of it, many believers were using their religious hypotheses in that way.

If so, there is no peculiar logical problem. An individual gets sick; this will be explained by saying that he has committed some great sin. Another individual has great success in his economic activities; again, religion will supply the explanation by supplying the general principle: for all *x*, if *x* is a faithful servant of religion, *x* will sometimes have great economic success. It may be noticed that if, in such explanations, words such as "sin," "faithful," and so on are used, the respective sentences do not need to be value sentences: they simply describe a way of behavior.

But it seems that such a way of explaining facts is alien to every more developed religion. In each of them the value element does play at least an important role.

2. The second case is one in which the hypothesis does not serve to explain factual sentences alone, but operates as a coordinator between the set of factual sentences and the set of value sentences accepted by the subject. It will then have a status similar to that of the postulate of existence of God in Kant, who found it necessary to admit the hypothesis of God in order to coordinate values *(summum bonum)* and facts. It seems that such a way of using the religious hypothesis occurs very frequently indeed. The classical application of this method is the solution of the problem of evil. The religious hypothesis allows the assertion that there is an afterlife, in which wrongs suffered in this life will be made good and so on.

But even though such cases seem to occur very

frequently, the logical structure of the reasoning used is practically unknown. The author is not able to offer, as yet, any solution of the problem.

3. Third, the hypothesis may be conceived of as explaining value sentences only. This is, as a matter of fact, a theory which has been often proposed by the theoreticians of various religions. In this case, the basis of our hypothesis would be constituted by the complete set of value sentences accepted by the subject. Factual sentences would play no role in its establishment.

It is, however, difficult to see how this theory would apply to our empirical material, namely, to the creeds of religions as they are and to the practice of the believer. For if the BD has to explain value sentences only, it seems that it must be a value sentence itself. But there is no known BD of such sort. Each of the empirically known BD's allows the drawing of at least some factual consequences, for example, that there is a God, that Reincarnation is a fact, and so on. Of course, great efforts have been made by theoreticians in order to show that all such sentences may be interpreted as pure value sentences, imperatives, and other such. It seems, however, that this does not fit the real situation and that such theoreticians misinterpret the behavior of the believers.

4. Finally, it is possible to conceive the religious hypothesis as explaining neither factual nor value sentences but sentences about particular religious

experiences. According to this view, the believers have had some specifically religious experiences and the class of sentences expressing them will be explained by the hypothesis.

Prima facie there is no logical objection against such an interpretation. The only question is whether there are specifically religious experiences—and this is an empirical problem. If it could be convincingly shown that this is the case, then it would remain to be shown what the structure of the reduction is.

As to the problem of prediction, this will be answered differently in each of the cases enumerated above. In case (1) the religious hypothesis will allow many predictions of exactly the same type as a scientific hypothesis. For example, a believer, observing that a son does not respect his father, will be able to predict that he will suffer much disadvantage in his career. In case (2) no direct predictions will be drawn from the hypothesis. It will only serve to coordinate, logically, the two fields in question. How this is to be done remains, as has been said, an unsolved logical problem. (3) When value sentences only are explained, predictions taking the same form will be made. Again, the logical structure is unknown, due partly to our lack of sufficient analysis of the field of values. Finally, it seems that, (4), a religious hypothesis explaining specifically religious experiences will allow the prediction of new religious experiences.

A final remark concerning these questions is this. As the content of the BD is the same as the content of the religious hypothesis, to know what the religious hypothesis explains and what it allows one to predict is relevant to the nature of faith itself and has, therefore, often been discussed. It seems, however, that most authors have taken for granted that there are only two possible cases, namely (1) and (3) above: religion is either a sort of science or exclusively a matter of evaluations. As a matter of fact, the situation looks far more complex than that. It offers, therefore, far more difficult logical problems than is usually assumed. Nor does assuming a situation to be simpler than it really is seem to be a convenient method of getting rid of such problems.

VI

Appendix

50. *Analysis of Analogy*

50.1 *Basic structures.* Analogy as discussed above (Section 38) is conceived of as a hexadic relation holding between two terms of the same shape, two things, and two properties of such things. In order to simplify the analysis, it will be assumed that this relation is always expressed in the same language l, so that the mention of that language can be omitted.

The general formula expressing a class of relations of the above kind is

50.11 $R(a, b, f, g, x, y),$

where "a" and "b" are to be substituted for by names of terms, "f" and "g" by symbols for properties, and "x" "y" by names of things. If we use "$S(a, f, x)$" for "a means f in x," we can define R as follows:

50.12 "$R(a, b, f, g, x, y)$" for "$S(a, f, x) \cdot S(b, g, x).$"

As we have $f = g \lor f \neq g, x = y \lor x \neq y$, and assuming that a and b are either of the same shape or not of the same shape (symbolically "$I(a, b)$ I $a, b)$,"), we obtain eight different relations of this kind. Their definitions may be schematically represented by the following table:

No.	a, b	f, g	x, y
1	I	$=$	$=$
2	I	$=$	$\neq$
3	I	$\neq$	$=$
4	I	$\neq$	$\neq$
5	$\sim I$	$=$	$=$
6	$\sim I$	$=$	$\neq$
7	$\sim I$	$\neq$	$=$
8	$\sim I$	$\neq$	$\neq$

This table should replace the old division of terms into univocal, equivocal (ambiguous), and synonymous (our numbers 2, 4, and 6). For our purposes, numbers 2 and 4 are of particular importance. We define them:

0.13   "$Un(a, b, f, g, x, y)$"   for   "$S(a, f, x) \cdot S(b, g, y) \cdot I(a, b)$
$\cdot f = g \cdot x \neq y$,"

0.14   "$Am(a, b, f, g, x, y)$"   for   "$S(a, f, x) \cdot S(b, g, y) \cdot I(a, b)$
$\cdot f \neq g \cdot x \neq y$."

50.2   *The semantic laws of excluded middle and of non-contradiction.* Two important laws may be derived by use of ordinary logical laws and rules from the above definitions. We call them "the semantic law of excluded middle" and "the semantic law of non-contradiction":

50.21 $(a, b, f, g, x, y): I(a, b) \cdot x \neq y \cdot \supset \cdot Un(a, b, f, g, x, y) \lor Am$
$$(a, b, f, g, x, y),$$

50.22 $(a, b, f, g, x, y): I(a, b) \cdot x \neq x \cdot \supset \sim [Un(a, b, f, g, x, y)$
$$\cdot Am(a, b, f, g, x, y)].$$

The first of these laws is important because it shows that a semantic solution of this kind cannot be a third relation in addition to univocity and ambiguity; it has to be, so it seems at least, one or the other.

This, however, holds only if f and g are taken to be unanalyzable wholes, as is usually assumed. If, on the contrary, the said properties could be analyzed, say f in φ and ψ, g in χ and ϑ, then the situation would be more complex and 50.2.1 could not be applied directly.

But this is what seems to happen when a word is used in a weakened meaning, as was suggested in Section 38. It is then possible to have a third situation in addition to univocity and ambiguity. And, as "analogy" was suggested as a name for such a situation, it can be said that analogy is neither univocity, nor ambiguity, but a third sort of relation.

This may be illustrated in the following instance: let "sees" be such an analogous word, and let us consider the two following uses of that word: (1) "John sees a cow here." (2) "John sees the truth of the first theorem of Gödel." Here we have two words of the same shape (namely, the two "sees"); we also have two different objects (namely, the cow and the theorem of Gödel), which are of course not identical. As to the properties concerned (here, the relations concerned) they are obviously different: the way in which one sees a cow is very different from that in which one sees the truth of a mathematical proposition. And yet there is something common in both cases.

50.3   *The nature of Analogy.* It is suggested that the common element mentioned is a certain set of properties common to both relations concerned. This implies:

1. That the properties concerned (f and g) are, in the case of analogy, always relations.

2. That they are different relations.

3. That they possess some common properties. The situation arising thus may be described in the following way. Our basic scheme must be changed to the extent that instead of absolute properties f and g we shall have relations, for example, R and Q; this being so, we shall have instead of two terms, four, or if one prefers, two couples of such terms; we shall write the symbols of the terms belonging to the same couple in square brackets. We can now define analogy as follows:

50.31   "$An(a, b, R, Q, [x, y], [z, t])$" for "$S(a, R, [x, y]) \cdot S(b, Q, [z, t]) \cdot R \neq Q \cdot [x, y] \neq [z, t] \cdot (\exists \alpha) \cdot \alpha(R) \cdot \alpha(Q)$."

The situation arising here may be represented by the following scheme:

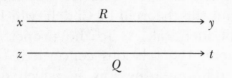

50.4　*Analogy as isomorphy.* It has been suggested in the body of the present work that analogy as used in RD is nothing else than isomorphy. This means that the properties common to both relations meant by the analogous words are the formal properties of these relations. By "formal properties" are meant such properties as can be defined by purely logical terms, for instance, reflexivity, symmetry, and transitivity. The definition of analogy becomes, if this suggestion is accepted, then:

50.41　"*An*(*a, b, R, Q,* [*x, y*], [*z, t*])" for "*S*(*a, R,* [*x, y*]) · *S*(*b, Q,* [*z, t*]) · *I*(*a, b*) · *R* ≠ *Q* · [*x, y*] ≠ [*z, t*] · *Smor*(*R, Q*)."

And the situation arising may be represented by the following scheme:

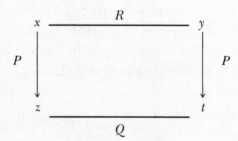

P is the correlator. This has to be, as is known, a one-one relation. Once such a correlator is given, all formal properties of *R* are properties of *Q* and inversely.

It is perhaps not impossible to conceive of analogy not as isomorphy, but as homoiomorphy, that is to assume a one-many relation instead of the one-one relation as correlator. This possibility would have to be investigated. As of now, it is certain that, for example, a syllogism *in Barbara* with an (or, more precisely, two) analogous term (terms) yields a conclusion; it is not certain if the same could be said about homoiomorphy.

The above suggestion recommends itself for the interpretation of RD because it permits the assertion of the "mysterious" character of the terms used to describe the OR, while not rendering the RD nonsensical.

50.5 *Historical remarks.* There exists an ample literature on analogy both in Catholic and in Brahmanic theology, and there have been great discussions about its correct analysis. Unfortunately, practically all such discussions have been conducted with quite inadequate logical tools, many authors (especially the modern) not even having the slightest idea about a logic of relations, which is quite obviously involved here. The situation was somewhat better during the Middle Ages, where some of the basic intuitions of Aquinas remain, it seems, the most solid things to be found in our field.

Only two among the many mistakes committed will be quoted here:

1. There was and still is a widespread doctrine according to which analogy should be basically thought of as a so-called analogy of attribution. This is the relation arising between two words meaning a state of affairs in one thing and its cause in another (for example, "healthful" referring to both an organism and to food). It is easy to show that whatever merits this concept may have, it certainly does not supply the possibility of reasoning about the OR.

2. Another interesting view was offered by Cardinal De Vio, who thought that the analogous terms meant a logical sum of two different properties, each of which belonged to one of the objects concerned. This theory does not suffer from the same handicap as the above; it has, however, some peculiar epistemological difficulties of its own.

The whole field merits far more attention than has usually been given it.*

51.1   *Analysis of Authority*

Formal Structure. Authority is a triadic relation between a person who has authority (and called here "authority"), another person, for whom the first one is an authority (this person will be called

*See the author's "On Analogy," in A. Menne, *Logico-Philosophical Studies*, Reidel, Dordrecht, 1962, pp. 96–117.

"the subject"), and a class of meaningful expressions, in regard to which the first is authority for the second (the term referring to this class will be "the field"). The formal structure of every authority is, consequently, this: x is an authority for (the subject) y, in (the field) α—symbolically:

(1) $A(x, y, \alpha)$

Being a triadic relation, A gives rise to three domains, and three partial (binary) relations with their converses. We have

$D_1 A = \hat{x} \, ((\exists\, y, a) A(x, y, \alpha))$	The authorities
$D_2 A = \hat{y} \, ((\exists\, x, a) A(x, y, \alpha))$	The subjects
$D_3 A = \hat{\alpha} \, ((\exists\, x, y) A(x, y, \alpha))$	The fields
$A^1 = \hat{x}\hat{y} \, ((\exists\, a) A(x, y, \alpha))$	The authority-subject relation
$A^2 = \hat{x}\hat{\alpha} \, ((\exists\, y) A(x, y, \alpha))$	The authority-field relation
$A^3 = \hat{y}\hat{\alpha} \, ((\exists\, x) A(x, y, \alpha))$	The subject-field relation

51.2   *Generalizations.* There are $2^3=8$ different generalizations of (1), and, when we take into consideration the various orders of the quantifiers, there are 12 more, that is, 20 altogether. By abbreviating (1) by "A" we obtain the following table:

2.1 $(x, y, \alpha)A$	2.5 $(\exists\, x)(y, \alpha)A$
2.2 $(x, y)(\exists\, \alpha)A$	2.51 $(y)(\exists\, y)(\alpha)A$
2.21 $(x)(\exists\, \alpha)(y)A$	2.52 $(y, \alpha)(\exists\, x)A$
2.22 $(\exists\, \alpha)(x, y)A$	2.6 $(\exists\, x)(y)(\exists\, \alpha)A$
2.3 $(x)(\exists\, y)(\alpha)A$	2.61 $(\exists\, x, \alpha)(y)A$
2.31 $(x, \alpha)(\exists\, x)A$	2.62 $(y)(\exists\, x, \alpha)A$
2.32 $(\exists\, y)(x, \alpha)A$	2.7 $(\exists\, x, y)(\alpha)A$
2.4 $(x)(\exists\, y, \alpha)A$	2.71 $(\exists\, x)(\alpha)(\exists\, y)A$
2.41 $(\exists\, y)(x)(\exists\, \alpha)A$	2.72 $(\alpha)(\exists\, x, y)A$
2.42 $(\exists\, y, \alpha)(x)A$	2.8 $(\exists\, x, y, \alpha)A$

51.3 *Intuitive Interpretations.* More important are the following intuitive considerations as to the nature of the entities referred to by the arguments of A. Here we have:

1. The authority itself is, basically, an individual. We may, indeed, talk about a social authority, that is, an authority of a class of individuals, but this may be easily constructed out of (1) where the first argument is an individual variable. It is also a person, an entity endowed with consciousness and, moreover, with the means of communicating the content of its consciousness to others.

2. The same applies also, basically, to the subject: this also is an individual person. Here, too, we may talk about a class, but primarily the second argument of "*A*" is taken to be an individual variable. The subject of authority must be, moreover, able to perceive and understand statements made by the authority.

3. The field of authority is a class of objectively meaningful utterances. By this is meant that it must be a class of utterances, that is, of symbols perceivable by the subject, of meaningful symbols, such as may be understood by him, and finally, that it must carry some objective meaning. Only objectively meaningful utterances may be accepted by the subject, and the acceptance of them seems to be essential to the authority.

So much for the arguments themselves. If we consider their mutual relations, we find the following state of affairs:

4. The authority must be distinct from the subject. It is, as a matter of fact, difficult to conceive that somebody may be an authority for himself; in some particular cases this can be proved. We have therefore:

51.31
$$(x, y, \alpha) \cdot A(x, y, \alpha) \supset x \neq y$$

Or, in other terms

51.32
$$A \in irr$$

5. The authority-subject relation is not transitive as such, that is, we do not have

$$(x, y): (Ez) \cdot A^1(x, z) \cdot A^1(z, y) \cdot \supset \cdot A^1(x, y),$$

but there are some (and even numerous) special forms of authority for which the above holds. Consequently this relation is not intransitive either.

51.4   *Social Authority.* Social authority, mentioned above, is twofold, for we may have an authority for a class of authorities and for a class of subjects. We shall denote the first by "*ACA*" and the second by "*ACS*." They may be defined as follows:

51.41   "$ACA(\alpha, y, \gamma)$"   for   "$(x): x \in \alpha \cdot \supset \cdot A(x, y, \gamma),$"
51.42   "$ACS(x, \beta, \gamma)$"   for   "$(y): y \in \beta \cdot \supset \cdot A(x, y, \gamma).$"

There may be also a "twice-social" authority, that of a class of persons for a class of subjects; this may be referred to by "*ACAS*" and defined

"*ACAS*" for "*ACA . ACS.*"

An instance of *ACA* is that of the physician for a sick man in the field of medical diagnosis and therapy. An instance of *ACS* is that of a ruler for his subjects in the field of their legal obligations. Finally an instance of *ACAS* is perhaps that of the authority of theoretical physicists for all cultivated men in the field of theoretical physics.

51.5   *Epistemic and deontic authority.* "*A*" can be analytically defined by using two other expressions, one meaning that *x* utters *P* with assertion in presence of *y*, the other, that *y* accepts *P*, the meaning of "accepts" being purposely left undetermined here. If we write "*U*(*x*, *y*, *P*)" for the first and "*Acc*(*y*, *P*)" for the second we have, as a matter of fact:

51.51   "*A*(*x*, *y*, *α*)" for "(*P*): *U*(*x*, *y*, *P*) · *P* ε *α* · ⊃ · *Acc*(*y*, *P*)."

However, the very vagueness of "accepts" obliges us to go now into a closer consideration of the nature of the field of authority. This, as was said, is a class of utterances carrying an objective meaning. It may be added that this meaning must be complete, since there can be no question of accepting an incomplete meaning. But there are two main classes of utterances carrying complete objective meaning, namely, sentences and imperatives. Accordingly, there are two main ways of accepting an utterance: a sentence will be accepted as true, or at least as possessing a certain probability, an imperative as binding. And if so, we have to deal with two quite different sorts of authority, according to the nature of their fields: the first one, that uttering sentences, will be called here "*epistemic* authority;" the second uttering imperatives, "*deontic* authority." The first will be referred to by "*AE*," and the second by "*AD*."

Much confusion seems to have existed and still does exist as to this twofold meaning of authority, and therefore a short example may prove helpful. Let us take the case of a lieutenant who is highly skilled in military science, and who is under the command of a rather unintelligent and uninstructed major.* This major is, for our lieutenant, a deontic authority in the field of imperatives concerning the war actions. He can command him for example to undertake an action Q, and the lieutenant has to accept this command as binding. But in our case the lieutenant is not bound to accept any sentence, not even the sentence corresponding to the command received: "the imperative prescribing Q is tactically justified." For only an epistemic authority can prescribe a sentence, not a deontic one. In other words, the epistemic authority is that of an expert, the deontic authority that of a commander or superior.

For our purpose only epistemic authority is of interest. We shall refer to deontic authority only incidentally.

---

*The author did hold that rank during the 1939–1945 war.

It is not implied that epistemic and deontic authority always occur in separate and distinct persons. On the contrary, the normal case, for example, in the army, will be that the same person is at the same time an expert and a commander. But it does not need to be so.

51.6   *Definition of Epistemic authority.* Why is epistemic authority accepted? Or, in other words, what happens when it is accepted? The answer is that, with the acceptance of such an authority, it is assumed that, whatever sentence is communicated by it in its fields, that sentence obtains a higher probability than it had before, the term "probability" being used here in its widest meaning, including the probability 1, that is, certainty.

More exactly what happens is this: at a certain time t_j a sentence P has, as related to the state of knowledge of y at the time t_j, a probability m; then at a time t_k (where $k > j$) x communicates to y with assertion P; then the probability of P as related to the state of knowledge of y at the moment immediately following t_k becomes n, where $n > m$.

If we wish to free this formula from the time variable, we may restate it in the following way: the probability of P as to the state of knowledge of y, which is s, and which does not include the knowledge of the fact that x uttered P, is m; but the probability of P as related to the product of s and of the sentence expressing the fact that x uttered P, is n, where $n > m$.

Now any of these formulae is not only implied by the fact that $A(x, y, \alpha) \cdot P \in \alpha$. It is equivalent to it; moreover, it seems that they mean the same thing.

If we abbreviate by "Q" the formula $U(x, y, P) \cdot P \in \alpha$, by "$Pr(P/h)$" the expression "the probability of P as related to h," and by "s" the expression "the state of knowledge of y without Q," we can now define epistemic authority in the following way:

(4) "$EA(x, y, \alpha)$"   for   "$(P) \cdot Pr(P/s) < Pr[P/(s \cdot Q)]$."

51.7 *Justification of authority.*   As has already been said (Section 46) there are two ways in which the acceptance of authority may be justified. The first way is that of insight into the person of the authority itself, as in the case of the mother. The second and, it seems, far more frequent, is by reasoning. It should be clear that this reasoning always has an inductive structure.

The simplest case is the following: y states that in so and so many cases sentences, belonging to the field, which have been asserted by x, have been later on verified as true; there are no or few negative instances, that is, cases in which x asserted a sentence belonging to the field and later on that sentence has been shown to be false. Then y generalizes and accepts the proposition, that, whenever $U(x, y, p) \cdot P \in a$, then P is true.

However, such a simple procedure seems to be seldom applied. Usually what we find is that some other arguments are used to justify the acceptance of authority. One such argument may take the following form: for all y, if y belongs to a certain class, then y is an authority in the field α: but a certain person A does belong to the said class; therefore A is an authority in α. This is surely the argument which justifies the acceptance of the authority of a physician or of a professor before any experience has confirmed their authority.

Here we have, however, to deal with social authority. Because A belongs to a class of persons endowed with authority in α, A is accepted as an individual authority in α. We must then ask how social authority is justified.

The answer is that the process is rather complex. It is inductive, from the experience of other members of the same class. And as premisses of that inductive reasoning, sentences are usually accepted which are again based in authority: for example, in order to accept the authority of a physician because he is a medical doctor, it is normal to refer to other persons who have been treated by other physicians and have had positive experiences with their authority. Consequently, reasoning justifying a social authority is complex.

51.8   *The probability of a sentence based on authority.* Except in the case of direct trust, the probability of any sentence accepted on authority is rather low. First, the justification of the main premiss, which ascribes a given authority to a person, is always inductive and such an induction cannot yield more than probability. But the probability present here is lower than that obtained by many other inductive reasonings because the premisses are often, as shown above, themselves based on authority.

Suppose that the probability of the product of such premisses is $1/m$; suppose again that the probability obtained by the rules of induction used is $1/n$ (where $n > 1$). It seems reasonable to admit that the probability of the conclusion will be less than either $1/m$ or $1/n$.

This being the case the scholastic rule *auctoritas est debilissimum argumentum* seems to be well founded. And if so, another old saying appears equally justified: *contra factum non valet auctoritas*. The latter means that whenever there is an inconsistency between a sentence P justified by any means other than authority and another sentence Q based, at least partly, on authority, P is to be preferred to Q. This seems to apply to any method of justification, by direct experience, by deduction, and by reduction. Of course, there may be cases in which a reductive justification of P is so weak that Q, based on a strongly established authority, must be preferred. But the normal case is the inverse one.

In the context of logic of religion this is interesting insofar as it supplies a strong argument against the confusion between rational justification by authority and faith; for, as was said above (Section 45), sentences belonging to faith enjoy a very high degree of probability, contrary to sentences based on human authority.

51.9   *The limits of authority.* Insofar as human authority is concerned, there are two obvious limitations to it.

The first is a limitation of the individual authority and consequently, of the social authority as well (because the latter depends on the former). It seems that for no human authority may the field variable be bound by a universal quantifier. In other words, every authority is only an authority in a limited class of sentences, not for all sentences. In that respect mistakes are very often committed, for example, when a physicist, because he is a good physicist, is thought of as having authority in philosophy or morals, and, inversely, when a philosopher, because he is a good philosopher, is believed to have authority in physics or sociology.

The second limitation regards social authority. It can be ascribed to a class of experts only on the condition that there is no basic disagreement as to the field under consideration among the elements of this class. For if there is such a disagreement, no element can enjoy authority because he belongs to a class. One interesting consequence is that a philosopher as such does not enjoy any authority, because philosophers disagree. This justifies the old rule in philosophy: *tantum valet auctoritas quantum allatum argumentum.*

An exception is, of course, the case when there is direct trust.

Index of Special Symbols

A, 163
ACA, 165
$ACAS$, 165
Acc, 166
ACS, 165
AD, 167
AE, 167
Am, 157
An, 159
BD, 1
LR, 1
F, 77
I, 157
M, 37, 113

OR, 1, 32
PD, 1
Pr, 159
π, 1
Q, 159
ρ, 1, 59
RD, 1, 10
S, 156
T, 77
TD, 1, 78
$\tau'\rho$, 1
U, 37
Un, 32, 157
Ut, 169

Index of Main Definitions and Theorems

1.1   Logic, its parts
1.21   Logic is about discourse
1.22   Logic is about objective structures
2.1   Conditions of existence of applied logic
2.2   Conditions of existence of applied formal logic
2.3   Conditions of existence of applied semantics
2.4   Conditions of existence of methodology
3.1   Religion a social phenomeneon
3.2   Religion comprehends discourse
3.3   Religion contains a Creed
3.4   A believer defined by acceptance of a Creed
5.1   LR not a part of Theology
5.2   LR auxiliary science of Theology
7.1   The criterion of authentic religion
7.2   Anti-logical and logical trends present
11.1   Theory of the Unspeakable not inconsistent
11.2   Theory of the Unspeakable not satisfactory
12.1   Non-communicativist theory discarded
13.1   Some parts of RD propositional
14.1   Formal logic applies to RD

15.1 Semantics applies to RD
16.1 Dialectics of little use for RD
20.1 Theological conclusions not obtained by
     deduction from
21.1 "God" a description
23.1 $E!\pi \cap \rho$
24.1 $\tau'\rho \subset -(\pi \cup \rho)$
24.2 $\exists!\tau'\rho$
24.3 $\exists!-\pi \cap -\rho$
25.1 $(\rho).F(\rho) \supset T(\rho)$
25.2 $(\exists\rho).\sim F(\rho).T(\rho)$
29.1 Believers support some determined ρ-sentences
32.1 Verification by authority not admissible
33.1 Verification by the BD, considered as
     hypothesis, not admissible
34.1 Direct verifiability necessary
34.2 Human view inconsistent with RD
36.1 Negative Theology discarded
37.1 Analogy is isomorphy
41.1 Insight theory of justification discarded
42.1 Some justification needed
42.2 Blind-leap theory discarded
43.1 Some justification of RD factually present
43.2 Justification of RD not quite conclusive
43.3 After justification an act of faith needed
43.4 Only after the act of faith the discourse
     becomes RD
44.1 Trust theory rejected under conditions
45.1 Purely deductive justification of RD impossible
45.2 Every justification of RD incomplete

47.1   Two sorts of crisis of authority
50.13   Univocity defined
50.14   Ambiguity defined
50.21   Semantic law of excluded middle
50.22   Semantic law of non-contradiction
50.31   Analogy generically defined
50.41   Analogy defined as isomorphy
51.41   Social authority (*ACA*) defined
51.42   Social authority (*ACS*) defined
51.51   Authority generically defined
51.61   Episthemic authority defined
51.9   Human authority limited

Index of Proper Names

Albert the Great, 22
Aquinas, 72, 161
Aristotle, 2, 3, 7, 46,
    72, 119, 139
Bach (J.S.), 27
Bellarmine (R.), 86
Cajetan, 162
Copernicus (N.), 86
Descartes (R.), 3, 4
De Vio (Th.), 162
Dignaga, 22
Frege (G.), 2
Galileo (G.), 86
Goedel (K.), 159
Husserl (E.), 94
Jevons (W. St.), 119
Kant (E.), 152
Kilimanjaro, 98

Luther (M.), 20
Lukasiewicz (J.), 119
Mohammed, 60
Neumann (Th.), 87
New York, 136
Peter Demianus, 20
Plato, 3, 7
Reichenbach (H.), 98
Russell (B.), 7
Savonarola (G.), 22
Scheiermacher (F.), 20
Stoics, 26
Tarski (A.), 13
Venus, 107
Whitehead (A.N.), 7, 24
Wittgenstein (L.), 27
Woodger (J.H.), 6
von Wright (G.H.), 6